For
Frances and Julia
with love

ACKNOWLEDGEMENTS

A version of Chapter 5 was published by BACP as 'Learning to be together alone' in May 2014 *Therapy Today*, Vol.25, Issue 4.

Part of Chapter 8 was published as 'How do I look?' in December 2014 *BACP Children and Young People* journal.

A version of Chapter 9 was published as 'Imprisoned in role' in June 2014 *BACP Children and Young People* journal.

I'm grateful to Kathy Peto, Professor Chris Mowles, Debbie Lee, Professor Jenny Pearce and Jane Campbell for reading and commenting on earlier drafts of this book. I'm also grateful to the hundreds of young people I've worked with over the years, to all my supervisees past and present, and to my own supervisor, Jane Campbell.

Thanks, as ever, to Kathy, Frances and Julia, without whom…

CONTENTS

1   Introduction   9

2   Sexuality in Schools   33

3   Five Boys and A Girl   51

4   My Body, My Self   71

5   Learning to be Alone   95

6   Shame and Privacy   107

7   Mothers and Fathers   129

8   Sexuality in the Counselling Room   149

9   Getting Stuck in a Role   181

10   Anger, Creativity and Sexuality   191

Endpiece   207

References   209

Index   215

1

INTRODUCTION

ELEANOR'S THIRTEEN. APPARENTLY she copes perfectly well with academic work, yet stays at home saying she's unwell and refusing to go to school.

'I think the real problem isn't bullying or anything like that,' says her teacher. 'I think it's anxiety... Any chance of you seeing her?'

As a counsellor, I see lots of young people who say they're suffering from 'anxiety', that they've had panic attacks, that they can't sleep, that they've been to the doctor and that the doctor says they might be 'depressed'. I know nothing of what's been going on in Eleanor's life, of her relationships at home or of what might have happened in the past. I do know, however, that when young people say they're 'anxious', they're usually describing a conflict – often an unconscious conflict – between how they feel and how they must behave, between wanting to remain a child and having to grow up. 'Anxious' usually involves having mixed feelings.

When we meet, she talks incessantly about her animals. She has all sorts; they all belong to her and they all need looking after. When I ask about her friends, she says she doesn't have any. Well, not really. At least, not any friends she sees out of school.

'My rabbit might be pregnant, though! I left her out in the garden but I think one of the wild rabbits might have got in through the fence...'

She tells me about the incubation period for rabbits and everything I'd ever need to know about baby rabbits. And baby guinea pigs. And hamsters. And mice. She doesn't talk about friends but seems to be using her animals the way other young people use their friends to explore the dilemmas of growing up. Two geckos don't like the third one she's put into their cage. Her grass snake might be lonely. Her new fish thinks he's the boss of the tank. For Eleanor, animals are evidently safer than people. She remains in control of the animals, apart – that is – from predatory male rabbits who sometimes get through garden fences intent on impregnating unsuspecting females. (Two years ago, Eleanor's mother left suddenly, going off with a local man.) Eleanor presides over a peaceable kingdom of animals who need feeding and cleaning out and who, she claims, rarely quarrel or fight or get jealous or break friends.

They do breed, though. Eleanor is clearly perturbed to think that she might not have adequately protected her female rabbit. I ask about boys at school.

'They're just silly,' she says. 'I don't take any notice of them.'

But you do worry about them, I think to myself. You probably worry about what they're capable of, Eleanor, and worry about how to control them in the future: whether to stay at home in your hutch, keeping well away from them, or whether to find some way of controlling them, some garden fence to keep them out. And what if they were to get through a fence, however well fortified? Could a fence ever be made impregnable? And what if one day there was a really nice rabbit out there somewhere who wanted to come in and play but couldn't get through the fence?

This book is about adults helping young people make better sense of sex and sexuality in order for those young people to feel less anxious and therefore less likely to act out their anxieties at their own or at other people's expense. However naïve Eleanor may appear to be, I've never worked with a thirteen-year-old person for whom sex hasn't been an issue affecting everything at some level: affecting everyday relationships with parents and peers, affecting a sense of worth, a sense of agency... Eleanor stays at home with her animals, anxiously cocooned, hoping that the world will go away but knowing that it won't. There are other thirteen-year-old young people who report that, unlike Eleanor, they're *never* at home, that they're always out with friends, sharing secrets with friends, breaking up with friends, making up with friends, ganging up on friends, helping friends with problems, arguing, getting bored, moving on, making new friends... Eventually one friend fancies another friend. They talk a lot and, before long, it's official: they're a couple. For two weeks. Then they break up and everything starts again.

'The paradox of sexuality', writes Phillips (1995), 'is that it both links us to other people and makes us feel at odds with ourselves' (p.91). There are young people like Eleanor who become aware of the sexual possibilities of life and keep their distance, approaching obliquely. For them, sex is somewhere up ahead, something to wonder and worry about on a long list of things to wonder and worry about. But there are other young people for whom sex is already happening. It's entertaining and exciting but also banal, risky and fraught with difficulty. This book describes the ways in which different young people get stuck and, with help, find ways of moving on.

'My cat doesn't like my rabbit! I think she's scared of it. But it's weird because she's got used to all the other animals and doesn't bother trying to get into their cages any more.'

Knowing cats, I express my surprise.

'As long as she's got someone to love her and stroke her, she's happy,' says Eleanor, intent on keeping our conversation away from the subject of people. 'She just doesn't like other animals getting too much attention!'

Eleanor is the eldest of three siblings. 'Your cat was your first ever pet,' I remind her. 'She's bound to be jealous of the other animals. She probably sees you looking after them and hates them getting all the attention!'

'No, I think she likes the other animals.'

'Okay, maybe she hates them a little bit ...'

'Maybe a little a bit.'

'Maybe it took away her confidence, Eleanor, when you started getting other animals? She was the eldest, after all. Maybe she became a bit of a solitary cat?'

Eleanor's not sure what 'solitary' means.

'I mean, maybe she decided that she was better off on her own? Not trusting other people?'

'You mean, not trusting other cats!'

I apologise for my mistake.

Like other developmental processes that young people must negotiate and survive, sexuality is unavoidable. In L.P. Hartley's famous novel *The Go-Between*, Leo is thirteen, like Eleanor, happily trying to please his friend's beautiful older sister until he discovers that she's merely using him to set up sexual trysts with the local farmer. Leo's childhood effectively ends with this discovery. 'I felt utterly deflated and let down: so deep did my disappointment and disillusion go that I lost all sense of where I was, and when I came to it was like waking from a dream' (Hartley 1953/1997, p.102).

Eleanor's mother is still living with The Man and Eleanor is waking fearfully from her own dream. Staying away from school is like trying to stay in her dream, in control of all her relationships, organizing the world so that people can't get hurt. For her, going to school would mean engaging with a world of betrayal, powerlessness, rivalry and sex (see Chapter 2). A world in which mothers run off with local men.

My experience of young people's struggles with sex and sexuality began as a teacher. Then later as a youth worker I tried to provide opportunities for young people to address these issues through informal conversations and structured group work. I remember doing my first condom demonstration. At the time, I couldn't get hold of any proper health education equipment, so I'd ordered a vibrator from a mail order company. But with anxious boys in mind and not wanting to make the boys feel any more inadequate than they might already be feeling, I'd ordered the smallest vibrator in the catalogue.

An opportunity presented itself. A group of thirteen-year-old boys were in the youth centre, joking about sex. I asked if they knew how to put on a condom. They looked at each other and giggled, meaning that, no, they hadn't a clue.

I fetched the box with the vibrator. They all watched anxiously until they saw it, then relaxed, visibly reassured. I felt pleased with myself.

I unwrapped a condom, emphasizing to the boys the importance of squeezing the teat 'So that the spunk stays tightly trapped inside and doesn't leak out anywhere...'

They nodded, all understanding.

I squeezed the teat and rolled the condom down onto the vibrator. Except that with the fully unrolled condom flapping against the sides of the vibrator, it dawned on me that this particular vibrator was far too small for demonstration purposes and, in fact, I'd gone and given the boys a whole new anxiety. Immediately they asked, 'How's the spunk supposed to stay in the teat?'

Sex is never the single most important thing in a young person's life, never the Freudian key that unlocks everything. But sex is always important, always a crucial means by which young people try to identify and understand themselves, regardless of whether or not they're in sexual relationships or on the brink of sexual relationships. Whatever their cultural background, young people find themselves surrounded by sexual images, by talk of sex, by other people's sex lives. Their bodies are changing in readiness for sex (see Chapter 4). Adults are increasingly reacting to them according to this new-found sexual potential and yet... And yet sex and sexuality are subjects that many adults (including counsellors, teachers and other professionals) are wary of talking about with young people. 'For clinicians, sexual love presents a special challenge,' writes Chodorow (1994). 'It is a fulcrum of gender identity, of sexual fantasy and desire, of cultural story, of unconscious and conscious feelings and fears about intimacy, dependency, nurturance, destructiveness, power, and powerlessness' (p.71). Most young people don't initiate conversations about sex any more than they initiate conversations about other difficult subjects. Instead, they rely on adults to anticipate and understand and do the asking. This book is about the dilemmas faced by those adults, especially by counsellors (as Chapter 8 describes), in trying to give young people opportunities to talk about and make better sense of their sexual experiences. It's a book about the pleasures and pitfalls of these conversations. It's about some young people like Eleanor who'll talk about sex obliquely, tentatively, while other young people will be raucous and rude (see Chapter 3).

Of course it depends on what we mean by 'sex' and 'sexuality'. As Foucault (1990, 1992) makes plain, our ideas about sex are culturally and historically determined. Attitudes change. Sexuality isn't a 'thing', is never fixed in stone and is always – in part – socially constructed (Nitsun 2006), its meaning shifting, with neuroscience shedding more and more light on the ways in which our sexual identities are formed, not only from biological predispositions, but from the impact on us of relationships (Hiller 2006). As Chodorow (1994) points out, '…men and women love in as many ways as there are men and women' (p.71). Nowadays, it might therefore be more accurate and inclusive to talk of 'sexualities', with words such as 'gay', 'straight' and 'bisexual' becoming unhelpful if, in fact, human beings are always positioning and repositioning themselves on a sexual continuum. Nowadays, our assumptions about gender are less fixed than they used to be (Hines 2007). Nowadays, the scene in which a thirteen-year-old girl called Juliet wakes up in bed with an older boy called Romeo would certainly be very different:

> ROMEO: It was the lark! I must be gone and live, or stay and die.

> JULIET: What are you on about?

> ROMEO: If I get caught with you, I'll be done for underage sex!

JULIET: You never asked how old I was…

ROMEO: Yeah, because you looked older!

JULIET: And you knew I wasn't on the pill…

ROMEO: No, I didn't! You never said!

JULIET: I shouldn't have to say! You should have used a condom.

ROMEO: They split!

JULIET: Yeah, 'course they do, big boy! Now I've got to go and get one of those emergency pills.

ROMEO: Where from?

JULIET: How should I know! Friar Lawrence maybe? Or some apothecary on the high street…?

For the purposes of this book, I take 'sexuality' to mean sex in its broadest sense: all the ways in which we relate to each other and express ourselves. I take it to mean our attractiveness to each other, the longing and sometimes repulsion that we feel for each other. 'Sexuality' might describe our psychological as well as our physical and social experience of each other, our 'biopsychosocial' selves (Hiller 2006), whereas 'sexual orientation' has a much narrower focus, describing only our attraction to one gender or another. Or both.

Adolescent sexual experiences are as formative as any other adolescent experiences. Some young people move confidently into adulthood but others take years to recover from the shame or the hurt of adolescence. As Chapter 9 describes, some get stuck, and with no help available, find themselves endlessly re-enacting their adolescent experiences, unable to move on. 'The sexual behaviour of a human being often lays down the pattern for all his other modes of reacting to life,' writes Freud (1908, p.198). This important idea might equally well be turned around: the way human beings react to their life experiences often lays down the pattern for their sexual experiences; if sexuality shapes our approach to life, then life shapes our approach to sex.

Counsellors and other professionals might talk a lot with young people about romantic relationships and might talk with some young people about sexual orientation. But who talks with young people about the sex bit? 'What will sex be like? Will I be any good at it? What will people expect of me? What about the things I don't know and don't understand? What if I don't like sex? How's it supposed to fit in with the rest of my life and the way I am with other people? Who can I talk to?' Friends can be unreliable witnesses and parents problematic for all sorts of reasons (see Chapter 7). So what happens if young people want to talk about sex and sexuality with their counsellors and with other supportive professionals but sense that it's somehow off-limits? What if they sense an unease in the professional? Who can they talk with then? Or are they obliged to muddle through, learning that this most intimate, personal and confidence-affecting part of their lives is to be negotiated alone?

Like other subjects that professionals avoid, I think that we avoid the subject of sex because of our own anxieties, including our paedophilic anxieties. On the one hand, we're aware of the collusive secrecy that leads to the sexual exploitation of children and young people, so we want to be as open and as honest as possible. But on the other hand we're aware that there are adults who befriend and groom children and young people through relationships built on trust. As professionals, we have to make relationships with young people and, as professionals, we hope to make trusting relationships. So what does it mean if we then go on to ask young people who trust us about their experience of sex and sexuality? Does it mean that we're being weird? Or prurient? Or paedophilic? Are we over-reaching ourselves? And yet if we say nothing, if we're always waiting for the young person to initiate the conversation, it might never happen and a young person's (potentially abusive) experience might remain a terrible secret.

Perhaps we worry that the subject of sex is best left to sex therapists. They, after all, have a specific training. They, in theory, should be better able to help. This may be true, but then presumably we'd also need to leave bereavement to bereavement specialists, stress to anxiety specialists and any sort of unexpected event to trauma specialists. The list would go on and on.

Perhaps we're wary of talking about sex with young people because of moral uncertainty. Should we be condoning underage sex, for example? Sex before marriage? Recreational sex? Homosexual sex? If there ever was, there's no longer any public consensus about sex and morality. And yet sex is always about morality, about the choices we make and their effects on other people, about kindness and cruelty, about our private and public lives (see Chapter 6). Counselling is also about morality. However impartial a counsellor might strive to be, her moral assumptions are always implicit in the things she says, the questions she asks. And the writer of a book will also be making moral assumptions.

So as a counsellor and as the writer of this particular book, I want to be explicit about some of my assumptions...

I think that loving sex is good and coercive sex is bad; that the sexual abuse of children and young people is a crime; that the quality of a relationship matters more than whether or not two people are having sex; that heterosexual relationships are no better or worse than homosexual ones; that there's nothing shameful about young people's sexual desire for each other and that it's perfectly possible for young people to have happy sexual relationships with each other.

I also think that when it comes to sex, young people have to make some mistakes in order to learn and become more resilient (Pearce 2007). Having said that, I can't help having my own view about what might be best for each of the young people I work with. I try to help them find their own solutions but I'll steer them if I think they're likely to get badly hurt or to hurt others. There are times when it's absolutely necessary for professionals to tell young people what they think. Going to break the windows of your ex-girlfriend's house is a bad idea. Going to apologize for breaking her windows might be a very good idea. I don't mean that, as a counsellor, I spend my time dishing out advice, but at the back of every young person's mind, sitting nervously in a counselling room, are important questions, 'Am I mad? Am I bad? Am I right? Am I wrong? What do you think?'

'Well,' I could say, 'what do *you* think?'

Turning the question back in this way, we might go on to have a useful discussion, but sometimes the question is still there at the end of a session with the young person feeling none the wiser. 'Am I mad or bad? Right or wrong? Please tell me! I need to know!' Of course there's a sense in which questions like these never go away and we just have to get used to them. But there are times when young people are overwhelmed by uncertainty and need the containment of someone who can offer a perspective. 'I don't think you're mad or bad,' I might say. 'I think that what you've said makes sense. I imagine that the people who don't know you very well wouldn't understand that the reason you lashed out isn't because you're stupid but was because you felt hurt by what you'd just found out about her. And your friends probably don't understand that the reason you've been avoiding them since then *isn't* because you're an unfriendly person but *is* because you've been hurt in the past and don't want to feel hurt again. It makes sense. You make sense! I'm not saying that you should hit people or take revenge on them for hurting you, but I *am* saying that you feel what you feel for a reason. Not because there's anything weird about you...'

In this way, it's possible to offer young people an understanding, a way of thinking about themselves that's helpful. And when it seems appropriate, I ask young people explicitly about their sexual relationships if I judge that the subject might be important:

'How are things with your boyfriend, Ryan?'

'Okay.'

'Is it sexual?'

'Yeah...'

'How's that going?'

'All right...'

'All right' is the answer that a lot of young people give, either because they've got nothing to compare the relationship with, so can't really say anything else, or because the sexual part of the relationship really *is* all right: not great, not terrible, a bit of a muddle...

'Does he love you?'

'He says he does...'

'And you believe him?'

'Sort of! He's really nice!'

'Sometimes it's hard to know what we feel about each other…'

'I know,' says Ryan, 'and I'm going to see how it goes. But it's all right at the moment.'

Lucy's different. She's forever complaining about her boyfriend: he talks to other girls too much; he won't talk about his feelings; he does whatever his mum says; sometimes he seems more interested in computer games… Every week we seem to be going over the same territory without moving on.

'How's the sex?'

'What d'you mean?'

'The sex… How is it when you're in bed together?'

She's taken aback but recovers herself. 'Pretty rubbish, if you must know…'

'Too much? Not enough? Not right?'

'Not right?' she says tentatively. 'At least I don't think it's right. I don't know. He seems happy enough, though.'

'But it might not be right for you?'

'It's just…' she begins. 'I don't know. This is embarrassing. It's just that he seems to think that once, you know, he's done his thing, that's it.'

'Like it's all about him?'

'Well he says he loves me and that,' she says, 'but he doesn't show it, if you know what I mean…'

'You mean, he has his orgasm and that's it?'

'Exactly!' She sits back in her chair. 'And I don't know whether to say anything. Obviously, I don't want to hurt his feelings, and I tell him he's really good at it but…' She laughs at herself. 'You know!'

'But he's not as good as he thinks he is?'

'Am I being stupid?'

I assure her that she's not being stupid and we go on to have a conversation about the necessity of teaching boys, explaining what feels good and what doesn't, what to do and what not to do.

When we meet again I ask how the sex has been.

She's happier. 'I did say a couple of things, you know, like we talked about, and he's really into it! He says it really turns him on!'

We continue to talk about her life, but with fresh purpose now. I'd never dream of approaching the subject of sex in so direct a way with most young people. But if I do ask, I ask in a similarly matter-of-fact way in order to cut through the embarrassment. With Lucy, I was fairly sure that we'd been circling the subject of sex for some time, going over and over the list of things she claimed to find so difficult about her boyfriend. Everything, it seemed to me, except sex. With her, I judged that our relationship was strong enough to cope with a conversation about sex and that, if necessary, she was perfectly capable of telling me to back off and mind my own business.

Occasionally, young people are brave enough to bring up the subject themselves. Imran mentions that his girlfriend never has an orgasm, which worries him, he says, 'In case I'm not doing it right.'

We discuss the fact of orgasm not necessarily being the sole indicator of good sex and discuss what Imran does and doesn't do with his girlfriend. In fact, he sounds like a remarkably attentive and well-informed sixteen-year-old lover.

'Maybe it'll be something that happens in the future,' I suggest. 'Maybe it takes time to get used to sex and to really trust a person...'

'But I feel bad,' he says, 'because I want her to enjoy it! I don't want to lose her! I really care about her!'

We go on to discuss the perennial problem of working out what we feel about other people and what they feel about us (Luxmoore 2010). We talk about whether or not his girlfriend actually wants to have sex in the first place. We talk about what it would be like to lose her and, almost inevitably, we end up talking about other losses in Imran's life, about what it feels like to be in a relationship and yet, at the same time, alone in the world (see Chapter 5).

Many young people like Ryan, Lucy, Imran and others in this book begin sexual relationships in their mid-teens. They're vulnerable to exploitation, abuse and violence (Barter *et al.* 2009), just as they're vulnerable to infection and pregnancy. They're also vulnerable to hurt and disappointment. But many of them are also capable of enjoying their sex lives and behaving very responsibly. As Phillips (1995) reminds us, it's important not to treat sex (and young people's sex lives) as a form of unhappiness. Sometimes the opprobrium directed at young people who are sexually active says more about the person directing the opprobrium than about anyone else. How much moral disapproval is really a cover for jealousy and regret? We might like to think of children and young people as innocents trailing clouds of Wordsworthian glory: kind not cruel, smiling not scowling, dreaming of princes and princesses rather than of how to inveigle each other into bed. But for *all* young people, regardless of their cultural background or intellectual ability, sexuality started happening ages ago, when they were babies discovering their genitals, when they were children asking about how they were made, when they started watching romantic films and wondering about all that kissing and lying back in bed covered by a sheet as if the film had just skipped over the really interesting bit. Again.

Psychotherapists would argue that sexuality begins at birth (Frosh 1999) through our first interactions with a mother, detaching from her yet wanting her, needing her yet biting her, screaming for her yet rejecting her. They would argue that the relationships we have with our parents are innately sexual, a collection of psychological and physiological experiences through which we begin to understand ourselves in relation to other people (Gomez 1997). In his famous study of sexuality, Freud (1905) writes that, in later life, 'the finding of a love object is always a re-finding' (p.222) because our first love object was and remains our mother. It may therefore be that a young person's sexual discovery through relationships with other people is effectively a sexual *recovery*, an unconscious attempt to recover something lost at birth, some promised land (Luxmoore 2011) or some 'primary tendency' we remember from infancy, whereby, as Balint (1935) describes it, 'I shall be loved always, everywhere, in every way, my whole body, my whole being – without any criticism, without the slightest effort on my part…', and this, Balint goes on, 'is the final end of all erotic striving' (p.63). Balint is describing the experience of so many of the young people I've worked with, frustrated by something seemingly always out of reach: 'Why can't he be the person I need him to be?' or 'Why won't she love me the way I deserve to be loved?' Young people are learning to bear the world as it is, while longing for the world as it could or should be. In his famous essay, Glasser (1979) characterizes this experience as the 'core complex' whereby a person must come to terms with his or her separateness from other people whilst, at the same time, experiencing 'a deep-seated and pervasive longing for an intense and most intimate closeness to another person, amounting to a "merging", a "state of oneness", a "blissful union"' (p.278).

In a sense, adolescence is always about searching for satisfaction while learning to bear frustration; about a primitive, out-of-control id doing battle with the censorious, controlling superego, presided over by an ego that gets into a muddle sometimes, that feels like giving up, that gets angry and vengeful, sad and lonesome, searching for love. 'The big problem about sex, the adolescent discovers, is that it is so pleasurable,' writes Phillips (2005). 'And this pleasure is initially revealed in masturbation' (p.139). Masturbation provides young people with a wonderful world of physical pleasure but then that wonderful world is quickly shown to be an illusion: no one's actually there. The need for physical pleasure and the need for attachment are inseparable for most young people. Masturbation is all very well, but the yearning for that wonderful lost world never goes away. Developing Bowlby's ideas, Diamond (2014) argues that 'Attachment and sexuality become fundamentally interrelated and overlie each other...' (p.270). 'There is a relationship between the quality of early attachments and the development of bodily experience, including sexuality...' (p.284). Importantly, she goes on to suggest that 'A human's capacity to link sexuality to a relationship is bound up with the quality of the attachment experience... Disturbances in early attachment relationships may correlate with difficulties in forming a relationship with a sexual partner in adulthood' (p.284).

In my experience, these early attachment disturbances are at the heart of so many young people's difficulties. As Chapter 7 describes, talk about a difficult boyfriend or girlfriend usually ends up as talk about a difficult father or mother.

Evolution suggests that we attach to survive, that we're attracted to a partner in order to propagate the species and that we start practising these processes from the very beginning of our lives as mother–baby sensuality develops into adult–adult sexuality. Writing about the very beginnings of our sexual experience, Fonagy (2001) describes sexuality as 'a genetically controlled physiological response that emerges within attachment contexts that are mutually regulatory, intersubjective, or relational' (pp.128–9). In other words, there's an inter-play between the raw genetic material of a baby and the relationships to which that baby is exposed. Our development as sexual beings is shaped biologically and environmentally. According to Freud (1905), we're all born 'polymorphous perverse', without any particular sexual orientation or identity, intent only on finding pleasure. Years later, Winnicott (1971) writes that, from infancy, men and women have a 'predisposition towards bisexuality' (p.72) while MacDougall (1995) identifies what she calls 'psychic bisexuality', a child's formative attraction to both a male and a female parent.

I find the idea of young people's initial bisexuality a helpful starting point: the idea that young people are all on a continuum, some more or less straight, others more or less gay. But because young people are defined from birth in terms of one thing or another – male or female, sporty or not, clever or not – they grow up expecting to define themselves as straight or gay. Developmentally, they're busy separating from their parents, no longer physically or psychologically merged but different, distinct. The possibility of bisexuality, therefore, like the possibility of being both dependent *and* independent, confuses and makes them anxious. So they redouble their insistence on being clearly defined for fear of losing their hard-won sense of separateness. With groups of young people, I sometimes use a very simple exercise (Luxmoore 2008). We go round the circle with each person completing the sentence that starts, 'One thing I'm *not* is...' No one can repeat what anyone else has said. We go round the circle at least four times. Then we switch to 'One thing I am is...' going round the circle a couple of times before starting a final round of 'One thing I'd like to be is...' The point is that young people can only move on to 'One thing I *am*' having first had plenty of chances to say what they're *not*. 'One thing I'm not' is safer, easier to say, whereas 'One thing I am' is more elusive, especially when 'who I am' is lots of different, sometimes contradictory things.

'I'm thinking about whether to get a sex change,' says Oliver, sitting down. 'I've been thinking about it for ages, but the doctor I went to see was useless. He told me it was just a phase I was going through! So then, last week, I went to see a different doctor and she'll help me if it's what I really want. The trouble is, I don't know if it is. Some days I definitely think I should do it, but then I get these doubts and I don't know if I should...'

Oliver's fifteen. There's nothing brash or impulsive about him. And he's done his research: he tells me that any treatment will be more effective the sooner he gets on with it. He asks what I think he should do.

I find myself wondering whether there's more to this than meets the eye, whether 'getting a sex change' is the tip of an iceberg, concealing other conflicts Oliver may be living with, conflicts about which I know nothing. Yet at the same time I'm aware of therapists pathologizing transgender issues, assuming that gender dysphoria must necessarily be a cover for issues to do with the past, with unsatisfactory childhood relationships, with identifying with one parent rather than another (Rattigan 2006).

'What do you think I should do?'

Our experience of the world is powerfully coloured by the gender we're assigned from the moment the midwife checks between our baby legs. Depending on our genitals, we're then encouraged to see the world in certain ways. As Butler (1990) argues, gender is socially constructed: we're taught to behave according to what's expected of a boy or girl. But the assumption that the gender to which we're assigned must therefore determine our futures (and future happiness) is unhelpful. Ideas about what's biologically 'natural' are also unhelpful: not everyone's genitals are conventionally male or female. Our individual biochemistry varies and neuroscience teaches that gender exists on a spectrum: distinguishing between 'male' and 'female' brains is far from straightforward (Baron-Cohen 2004; Hines 2004; Jensen and Ellis Nutt 2015). In my experience, young people like Oliver start asking questions about their gender and sexuality because they're being honest with themselves rather than perverse.

'What do you think I should do?'

I take a deep breath. 'I think you're asking good questions, Oliver. None of us should be forced into little boxes just to keep other people happy. And I suppose there's also the question about whether we need to be one gender or the other. Why can't some people be both? Or neither? Or changing? Nowadays some people describe themselves as "queer", meaning that they refuse to be defined as one thing!' 'I know!' he says, excited by this. 'And that's why I'm not sure! If I'm a boy and I want to be a girl, do I have to have the operation or can I just be a girl, wear girls' clothes, go where girls go, do what girls do? And the thing is, I'm not sexually attracted to boys or girls. Well, not at the moment. I like girls but I don't think about having sex with them!'

I want to applaud his open-mindedness about these things. But one young person's open-mindedness is another's terror: for most young people, it's frightening not to know exactly how they fit in with other people. Most young people live in search of certainties (Luxmoore 2014).

'You still haven't said what you think I should do!'

'That's because I don't know,' I say. 'I don't know what you should do. But I think not knowing is okay. People are always trying to make us decide about things because it makes their lives simpler. I think you should continue with not knowing for as long as you want!'

'But what if I need an operation?'

Oliver gets on with his parents and two sisters at home but, so far, hasn't begun to have this conversation with them. I tell him that only about a third of all transgender people have surgery. We agree to keep meeting and talking about all these things; we agree that he'll keep talking to the sympathetic doctor and that, at some point, he'll probably have to find a way of talking with his parents, daring to ask them what they think.

Counselling with young people is always about developing a sense of identity, but an identity that's more flexible and nuanced, more open to possibility than the narrower identity most young people have adopted in their initial strivings to be distinct. This makes the processes of counselling scary for many young people, with the processes of love and sex also threatening to undo their fixed sense of identity. A boy might have been in trouble with school and with the police, for example, driving his mother to distraction. Then he starts going out with someone and his long-suffering mother is delighted. 'He's been a different boy ever since they've been together!' she says. Other parents might report an opposite experience: 'It's only since the two of them have been together that the trouble's started!' As Chapter 9 describes, it's comforting to play a distinct role, knowing exactly what's expected of us. It's comforting but also terribly restricting. New experiences like counselling and like sex are nerve-wracking but potentially transformational. On a good day, young people might leave the counselling room as they might leave the bedroom, feeling competent and interesting, attractive, unafraid, sated, affirmed. But on a bad day, they might leave feeling fragmented, misunderstood, frustrated, as if all those old baby anxieties have come flooding back: 'No one cares about me! No one loves me! No one wants to be with me!'

So what of Eleanor, fixed in her determination to stay at home, controlling her animals? Bettelheim (1976) describes the ways in which fairy tales about animals ('The Frog Prince', for example) often explore unconscious sexual anxieties. Sometimes Eleanor and I talk about sex and sexuality through the metaphor of her animals, wondering about their relationships with each other, their motivations and rivalries, the extent to which they're powered simply by the need to reproduce and the extent to which the animals might have feelings about each other. Sometimes Eleanor shuts down the conversation abruptly, insisting that an animal is just an animal, that there's no subtext, no difference between appearance and reality. Occasionally we talk about The Bad Mother who went off with The Man, changing everything in Eleanor's life, and as the weeks go by, she allows this conversation to develop a little. We think about her parents' relationship before the split, about her mother as a person and whether there might be good things about her mother as well as all the bad things Eleanor is normally so quick to list.

One day I say to her, 'Maybe your mum just fancied him, Eleanor?'

'She shouldn't have, though, should she! Not if she was married to Dad!'

'Maybe not, but sometimes people can't help themselves. They know they shouldn't, but they do…'

She thinks about this.

'Do you think it makes your mum bad? Or do you think it makes her brave in some ways? Especially if she felt that she didn't love your dad any more?'

She's thinking about this, but it's scary. She looks away. 'After school I'm going to buy some more food for my budgie.'

2

SEXUALITY IN SCHOOLS

A VERY FAMOUS psychoanalyst is remembering his teachers...

> We wooed them or turned away from them, we imagined sympathies or antipathies in them that probably did not exist, studied their characters and formed or distorted our own on the basis of theirs. They provoked our greatest levels of rebelliousness and forced us into complete submission: we sought out their foibles, and we were proud of their preferences, their knowledge and their justice. Basically we loved them very much if they gave us any reason to: I do not know whether all our teachers noticed that. But it cannot be denied that we faced them in a very special way, a way that might in some respects have been uncomfortable for them. From the outset we were equally disposed to love and to hatred, to criticism and to worship of them. (p.355)

Reading Freud (1914) on his schooldays, it's hard not to hear the sexual undercurrent, the intensity of a boy's feelings about his teachers, facing them 'in a very special way, a way that might in some respects have been uncomfortable for them'.

Because schools are full of young people, they're full of sexual anxiety and desire. Over the decades, education has traditionally been used as a way of regulating that desire. All those cold showers! All those cross country runs! In schools, the talk is constantly of teaching and learning in the classroom, of the exciting futures awaiting students who work hard and get good exam results. It's as if the school year builds gradually, gradually, gradually to an orgasm of exam results with dozens of young people finally leaping skywards.

But if passing exams is the official school task, there are plenty of unofficial tasks. As far as most young people are concerned, making and keeping friends is a far more important task. And lurking at the back of their minds are other, equally important preoccupations: how to replace sexual curiosity with sexual confidence; how to bear the sexual frustration building up inside. Yet these things remain hidden under an exam radar busily scanning the classroom for signs of inattention and under-performance.

So when Cassie comes to see me, I have no idea why. She seems to have plenty of friends, works hard, gets top grades and is expected to do well in all her exams. She seems to have no problems at school and her family is happily muddling through at home.

I ask about all these things, wondering whether she feels taken for granted, a victim of the fact that, whereas trouble attracts attention, young people like Cassie who get on with their lives uncomplainingly get little attention. Perhaps she's come to see me because she needs to know that she's interesting, even without an obvious problem.

At the end of our session, I suggest that we meet again and she looks relieved. Only when we meet for the second time do I begin to understand. This time we talk about some of the boys she knows and about how she almost fell out with one of her best friends, Susannah, because she was talking to Susannah's ex-boyfriend at a party and Susannah became suspicious.

'There was nothing going on,' says Cassie. 'All I was doing was talking to him. I don't see what's wrong with that!'

We both know what *could* be wrong with that, if Susannah had recently split up with the boy, and if Cassie was thereby breaking the girl-rule whereby you don't go near someone's ex-boyfriend or girlfriend until a certain amount of time has elapsed. 'The thing is, they split up ages ago,' she says, 'so I don't see what's supposed to be so wrong!'

I ask if the boy fancied her.

'I don't think so,' she says. 'We were just talking.'

'But he liked you?'

She looks wary. 'He might have liked me a bit. But that was all.'

'It's nice to be liked, Cassie…?'

'Yeah,' she says, pulling a strand of hair away from her face, 'I'm not denying that.'

'And nice to be fancied…?'

She makes a modest, non-committal face, but then smiles with satisfaction, and I begin to understand something about why sensible, hard-working Cassie has come to see me. I suggest to her that, if most people see her as academic and well-behaved, it must be lovely to know that she's much more than they realize: that she's also attractive and desirable, the sort of girl people would want to go out with.

She admits that, yes, this would be nice, if it were true.

We continue to meet, integrating old, sensible Cassie and new, sexual Cassie: allowing her to acknowledge and enjoy this newly discovered sense of herself without embarrassment and without having to ask anyone's permission. Over time, she gets invited to more parties, which inevitably causes consternation at home. She starts wearing make-up and little studs in her ears. But throughout these changes in her life, she continues to work hard at school while enjoying the excitements of this new life away from school.

Cassie's unusual. The academic learning of most young people is interrupted by sexual anxiety. Who fancies whom? Who's talking or not talking to whom? Who's worrying about being left on their own? Who's started going out with whom and who's just broken up with whom? Who's quietly waking up to the charms of the person sitting on the other side of the classroom? Who's doing it with whom? Who's secretly living with an experience of sexual abuse? So much is going on in young people's lives. Reliable research in the UK (Radford *et al.* 2011) reports that, of a large sample, 0.5 per cent of children under the age of 11 had experienced 'contact sexual abuse' as defined by the law. Amongst young people aged 11–17, the percentage rose sharply to 4.8 per cent (one in twenty), and amongst young people aged 17–24 the percentage was 11.3 per cent (at least one in ten). Sixty-five per cent of the reported abuse was perpetrated by children and by young people themselves.

Schools might talk about preparing young people for the outside world, but that doesn't mean preparing them as sexual beings. Officially, this is left to parents or – more probably – to chance. I'm not advocating the abandonment of rigorous learning in favour of some sexual free-for-all, but in my experience academic learning is more effective when there's an acknowledgement of these undercurrents. Pretending otherwise is counter-productive. 'Concentrate on your schoolwork!' is all very well but has little effect on young people in love, young people potentially in love, young people who've just fallen out of love or young people coping with their first sexual experiences. Better to find opportunities for young people to talk about these things because, having talked, it might then be possible to concentrate on schoolwork again. Klein (1975) writes that 'school and learning are from the first libidinally determined for everyone, since by its demands school compels a child to sublimate his libidinal instinctual energies' (p.59). If, as Klein (1991) argues elsewhere, we have an 'epistemophilic' instinct, an instinct to find out, an instinct for knowledge, then that knowledge inevitably includes sexual knowledge. Learning is never a purely cerebral activity.

The more we repress sexuality in schools, the more problematic it becomes. Yet members of staff will rarely talk explicitly about sex and sexuality, however pervasive these things may be. All around school there'll be men dressed in suits, giving little away, careful about how close they stand to other people; there'll be women allowed more sartorial leeway but nevertheless wearing clothes chosen to deflect attention away from their bodies. There'll be hundreds of students in uniform, determinedly expressing their ambivalence about having to look like everyone else, conforming in some ways but, in other ways, challenging the norm at every turn with clothes that are too tight or too revealing, with piercings, jewellery, haircuts, make-up. On every day of the school year, battles are fought over the minutiae of these things. And there'll be students challenging the norm through their language and behaviour: through sexual swearing, through sexual remarks and innuendos, through sexual touch, some of it permitted (holding hands, polite kissing), and some of it forbidden (hands creeping under clothes). In some schools, even holding hands is forbidden. As Briggs (2008) has it, 'Sexuality as well as happiness gyrate around the centrality of the educational attainment discourse, generating meaning, self-esteem and developmental crises' (p.46). In that sense, Cassie – an academically successful student – isn't unusual in struggling to weigh the importance of her discoveries away from school against the familiarity of her life in school. It would be impossible but it would be simpler if Cassie could keep her academic and sexual lives quite separate. In the UK, there are still old school buildings with 'Girls' carved over one entrance and 'Boys' over another. From time to time, debates about the pros and cons of single-sex education recur, with the proponents of single-sex education arguing passionately that young people are less likely to be 'distracted' from their academic work in a single-sex school. The possibility that sexuality might be just as powerful a distraction in a single-sex school is lost in a fantasy of the heterosexual coupling inevitably unleashed if ever boys and girls are left alone together.

Eros and Thanatos are powerfully present in school life: sex and the repression of sex, the libidinal id and the anti-libidinal superego. I remember hearing about a girls-only school where a group of older students wanted to set up an LGBT (lesbian, gay, bisexual, transgender) group. Frantic discussions took place in the staffroom with teachers worrying that any younger girls attending the group might be 'influenced'. The suggestion was put forward that students from the local boys' school might also be invited to join the LGBT group. This might well have been an enlightened suggestion from someone wanting to make the group available to as many young people as possible – wonderful! – but I suspect that it was probably put forward in the hope that the presence of boys would necessarily promote a more heterosexual culture in which any younger girls would be less likely to be 'influenced' because they'd necessarily be reminded of the attraction of boys.

For over ten years I ran the sex education programme in one secondary school. In the beginning, there was almost no provision: a few half-hearted, uncoordinated lessons about the birds and the bees framed by vague injunctions to 'respect other people' and 'be safe'. So with a few colleagues I set about instituting something more robust that answered students' questions, especially the questions they were too shy or too cool to ask (Luxmoore 2010). Eventually (as Chapter 3 describes) we developed something that was frank, age-appropriate and not just about heterosexual sex. But the most important reason for developing this work wasn't simply to supply students with information, important though that was: it was to affect their everyday behaviour with each other, because if sexual relationships remain mysterious and shameful, then young people will be uneasy and will mock each other; if homosexual sex can't be talked about, then there'll be homophobic bullying; if sex is off the curriculum, as it were, then there'll be non-stop conversations about sex, non-stop anxieties about sex and a non-stop acting out of these anxieties. Good sex education doesn't delay the age at which young people have their first sexual experiences but does tend to make young people more responsible and emotionally committed within those sexual relationships (Graham 2004).

I remember starting work as the counsellor in a school where there had never been a counsellor before. Two thirds of the teachers were male and two thirds of these male teachers were over fifty. There was plenty of casual bullying in the corridors and most teachers fled to the staffroom at break times. A new headteacher had recently been appointed who had started to change things, but there was still much talk in the staffroom of the good old days when, apparently, students knew their place. Several members of staff told me they thought that the school disciplinarian, a military man who'd taught at the school for 35 years, should have become the new headteacher.

My arrival as someone keen to say hello and talk with students around school, indeed as someone whose *job* was to talk with students about how they were feeling, caused consternation among the older boys in particular who were used to the male supremacy of a quasi-military regime. After a few weeks I started hearing the word 'queer' whenever I appeared and before long 'Queer!' was being growled or shouted out in disguised voices whenever I was near, always from the shelter of a group, so that the person shouting couldn't be identified. 'Queer! QUEER!'

Needless to say, there was no official recognition that this or any other kind of sexualized bullying was a problem in the school. New members of staff were expected to 'tough it out'.

To ask for help was a sign of weakness and to challenge the prevailing culture was clearly to have no sense of humour.

I bore all this as best I could by toughing it out, by doing my best to get to know the boys *and* by challenging the culture. After a few years the culture began to change for the better. But what was interesting was that the arrival of a counsellor had provoked such *sexual* anxiety. Out had come the homophobia! Out had come the misogyny! Out had come the frantic male bonding! It was as if the very idea of counselling had threatened the boys (and undoubtedly some teachers), all desperately hiding behind their macho facades. For them, sexuality was about male domination, conformity and shame. Counselling was allegedly about being gay and being gay was too dreadful to contemplate.

The sexual undercurrents in a school also find less overt expression. A school dance show, for example, might unwittingly chart young people's transition from sexual innocence to experience. The evening might typically begin with dozens of eleven-year-olds in leotards and football kits enthusiastically performing a series of conventional, aerobic, keep-fit routines. They go off stage to resounding applause and are replaced by a class of embarrassed thirteen-year-old students (almost all of them girls) who perform a miscellany of moves drawn from ballet, cheerleading and music videos. They finish to sympathetic applause and an exam group of disgruntled fifteen-year-olds takes to the stage. They've been let down at the last minute by a few of their number who've stayed away to tend to a surprising number of sick relatives ('How would you like it if your nan was dying?'). The students who've turned up perform a piece they've devised called 'The Seasons', beginning with 'spring' in which two students are obliged to move around in ways suggesting that they might be attracted to each other and that some kind of union is in the offing. The two students involved studiously avoid looking each other in the eye and are clearly relieved eventually to be joined on stage by the rest of the group who move about in ways indicative of 'summer' but avoid any hint of sweaty sexuality by concentrating instead on the hot weather, on trees basking in the sunlight and on small animals scurrying around. The piece finishes ('It all went wrong!') and the students slope offstage to be replaced by a well-organized group of older students, all wearing black, all looking glamorous and confident, performing routines suggestive of altogether darker things, routines that seem to involve chasing each other around, touching each other a lot, falling into each other's arms at regular intervals and finally lying prone together on the stage, exhausted, panting, enjoying the applause.

In a school, choosing the annual musical production is another matter of delicate sexual balancing. Do we perform *Grease* or go for a less overtly sexual option? Will whoever plays Sandy be able to transform herself from well-behaved virgin to knowing, leather-clad siren? Will the students playing Rizzo, Kinecke and the rest have the necessary sassiness to carry it off? Or would it be safer to do *Oliver* again this year?

In schools, it's hard to acknowledge these undercurrents, however pervasive they may be. No one wants to embarrass or shame students by naming things that some of the students themselves have barely named. Yet pretending that schools are not highly sexualized places makes it harder for young people to make sense of their experience, especially when longing turns to lust.

I remember some years ago, the news was full of it. A schoolgirl had run off with one of her teachers. At first there was the worry that the teacher might have killed her but then the story changed as CCTV pictures showed them arm-in-arm as they left the UK on a ferry to France. Now they were probably hiding somewhere in France, perhaps in a cheap hotel, perhaps sneaking out for walks together, kissing and who-knows-what else… A fifteen-year-old girl and her thirty-year-old lover.

In the schools I visited, everyone was talking about it because everyone, I suspect, had an investment in the story. Every student had imagined the romance of falling for a teacher and every teacher had imagined what it would be like to run off with a student. For as long as the story ran, the schoolgirl and her teacher were the objects of everyone's vicarious interest. What would happen next? Would they be caught? Would their relationship last?

I don't know how many of the teachers would have publicly admitted to their interest in this story, however. In Germany, Italy and Portugal the age of consent is fourteen; in France, Denmark, Sweden, Poland and Greece it's fifteen. In the UK, sex with anyone under the age of sixteen – however consenting – is illegal and any sexual relationship between a student and teacher leads to the teacher's instant dismissal. I'm not for one moment challenging the rightness of this. Of course teachers are in positions of trusted authority and of course they'll sometimes be the objects of student desire. They must never abuse that authority or compromise their delicate role in the lives of young people. Of course!

What I *am* challenging is the implication that good, responsible teachers won't have feelings for students which will sometimes be sexual. They will. It goes with the territory. Indeed, it can happen from time to time in any profession where the relationship between people is the key to getting the job done. It doesn't mean that these feelings of attraction will necessarily be acted out: there are important boundaries that mustn't be crossed. But these boundaries become more blurred and teachers are more likely to get into a muddle and end up crossing them if they have no way of talking about and beginning to make sense of the feelings they find themselves experiencing. Once the possibility of intimacy between students and teachers has become a taboo subject, the experience becomes shameful with teachers obliged to hide and hate their feelings. But if those feelings can be acknowledged and talked about as inevitabilities rather than as signs of weakness or perversity then teachers are more (rather than less) likely to remain in control of the situation and not cross any boundaries.

Teachers, priests, youth workers, social workers and counsellors are parent-figures whether they like it or not. This adds to the confusion because, again, it's illegal for parents to have sexual relationships with their children. It's hard for parents ever to talk about the sexual feelings they may nevertheless have for their children. I don't mean genital desires. I mean their feelings at the other end of the sexual continuum – benign feelings of admiration and attraction, from the mother who says she wants to bite her baby's peachy bum to the father who fondly strokes his daughter's hair. Parents think that their children are beautiful and want to protect them from the sexualized staring of strangers.

But they only become aware of their child's attractiveness to others because they themselves are aware of their child's attractiveness.

Some parents are perfectly comfortable with this but others find the whole experience disturbing. There are fathers who respond to their daughters' burgeoning sexuality by suddenly keeping a physical distance and deriding their daughters' best attempts to look glamorous. The daughters, for their part, unable to attract the benign admiration of their fathers, are obliged to look for admiration elsewhere, often with disastrous consequences, and all because their fathers are afraid to acknowledge the beauty (including the sexual beauty) of their daughters because it feels too unsafe, weird, shameful, paedophilic. There are step-fathers beset by the same worries. And there are other adults (a mother's boyfriend, for example) who, coming into the life of a family, find themselves failing to connect with a teenage son or daughter and wondering why. Fathers and father-figures often attack in daughters what they can't acknowledge in themselves.

As parent-figures, teachers can end up feeling similarly confused and scared, thinking, 'I shouldn't be having these feelings. They're wrong! I must be a bad person!' Sometimes important relationships with students are abruptly curtailed because the teacher gets frightened and – crucially – feels unable to ask for support from other professionals for fear of sounding perverse and unprofessional. The student is left in emotional limbo, feeling guilty of some unspecified crime.

A long time ago, Suttie (1935) argued that there existed a 'taboo on tenderness' whereby the tenderness between a parent and child was deemed babyish and weak. The result, he observed, was a 'psychic weaning' that effectively split tenderness apart from sex. Sex became a socially acceptable goal for boys and men, he argued, while tenderness was scorned as unmanly. Decades later, I wonder how much this is still the case. How much are we still unable to conceive of tenderness and sex together? How much do we still fear that a display of tenderness will automatically lead to sex or that the tender person is always plotting a sexual outcome? How difficult does it therefore become for a teacher, counsellor or other professional to express feelings of tenderness towards a young person for fear of what might happen? And if tenderness and sex *are* always on a continuum, who helps the professional to make sense of these things so that people don't get hurt?

The schoolgirl and her teacher were eventually found and returned to the UK where the teacher went to prison. But if only he'd talked to someone about what he was experiencing. If only the taboo on talking about these things hadn't forced their relationship to remain secret…

A few years later, I was listening to a conversation about the case on the radio. Apparently the teacher's parole hearing was imminent and the story was still clearly of interest to many people. Except that now it was different. Now the story being told was of a manipulative man who had quite deliberately and callously groomed a schoolgirl for his sexual satisfaction. In this new story, there were no grey areas: he was the perpetrator and she was the victim.

I know nothing about the detailed facts of the case. But I was interested that the narrative changed from one about a young person and her teacher in love to a much simpler story about a predatory adult preying on a helpless fifteen-year-old.

In the new story, the girl lost all sexual agency: she was a child; he was an adult; she was asexual; he was sexual. Simple as that!

As I say, I'm not condoning the sexual abuse of young people or any professional's abuse of power. What I am suggesting is that it's rarely that simple: human sexuality is complex and young people are sexual beings. To pretend otherwise risks driving their experience underground, making abuse more rather than less likely. I run training sessions in schools where members of staff sometimes say, 'We've been told that we're not allowed to be alone in a room with a student!' Seeing my bewilderment, they go on, 'It's because a student could allege anything and there'd be no witnesses and then where would we be?' In this story, all students are predators, intent on taking sexual advantage of unsuspecting members of staff: a story again simplifying the complexities of sexuality to a fairytale about Evil Predators and Helpless Victims. The same members of staff never say, 'We can't be alone in a room with a student because we might find ourselves attracted to the student and then where would we be!' It's worth noting that, in most schools, despite the fact that all members of staff have been officially checked to make sure that they're 'safe' to work with young people, staff and student toilets are clearly marked and kept quite separate. There may be perfectly good reasons for this, but I've often wondered whether there's also an unspoken concern that sharing the same toilets might lead members of staff and students on to other intimacies.

If schools are like enormous families, containing and bearing witness to the emerging sexuality of so many young people, then just as children will take their cues from parents, students will take their cues from members of staff. They'll notice, for example, how members of staff greet each other. Do teachers call each other by their first names, or do they insist on referring to each other as Mr. Smith and Mrs. Brown? Are Mr. Smith and Mrs. Brown pleased to see each other and how do they show that? Do they ever hug? What are school celebrations like? Are they ritualized and predictable or participatory and fun? How do members of staff handle their particular friendships with each other? Are these friendships kept secret or publicly acknowledged? How *playful* are the adults in school allowed to be?

Because sexuality *is* essentially playful and unpredictable, the ways in which schools allow or don't allow for young people's sexuality will be informed by the ways in which they allow for and are able to live with the unpredictability of daily life, insisting either on endless bureaucratic protocols or managing to live with the fact that, on any given day, anything might happen. Teachers are understandably ambivalent about this. They'll often claim to enjoy their jobs because 'No two days are ever the same and you never know what's going to happen!', yet will typically spend their evening hours trying to ensure that the following day is as predictable as possible.

Of course, structure and spontaneity are both important for young people. In some families, sexuality is a guilty, shameful secret that mustn't be spoken about, while in other families, sexuality spills out everywhere and everyone knows everyone else's business. Neither model on its own is helpful for young people, and schools, for their part, need to be both structured and spontaneous. It's just that when it comes to sexuality, so many schools get scared and fall back on structure at the expense of spontaneity.

A young person's anxiety or confidence develops in the context of a family and a school. If 'school' is always an unconscious mother or father, as I've argued elsewhere (Luxmoore 2014), then what messages about sexuality does a particular school emit? I share Nitsun's (2006) view that sexuality is an important connecting, bonding part of any group experience. In schools where sexuality is repressed and bureaucratized, my experience is that young people feel less able to connect with each other in public. They're forced to find ways of connecting in secret (quietly cutting their arms, for example, and sharing that experience online), or to find overly dramatized ways of connecting, publicly drawing people to them through extremes of anti-social behaviour.

Over the years, my work has involved trying to promote cultures in schools where anxieties about sex and sexuality are diminished, where members of staff feel better able to be spontaneous and where young people feel better able to connect safely and happily with each other.

Sometimes that work has been through sex education...

3

FIVE BOYS AND A GIRL

WITH A TEAM of health professionals, I'm running a weekly lunchtime drop-in clinic for young people in school as part of my job as the school counsellor. Officially, the clinic offers advice and information about anything from spots and dieting to giving up smoking and managing periods. Unofficially, the vast majority of young people using the service come with a keen interest in sexual health and, in particular, contraception.

Three boys approach me in the corridor. They're about fourteen years old, smiling and hoping that I'll guess what they want without them needing to say.

Guessing is extremely easy. 'Condoms?'

They smirk, bravado mixed with embarrassment as I shepherd them into a side room. Suddenly there are six of them, including one girl.

Regardless of whether or not they're in sexual relationships, I'll give each of the boys a couple of condoms. If I ask, they'll all claim to be deeply immersed in sexual relationships anyway. 'And there's a party this weekend,' they'll say, 'so we're *definitely* going to need some johnnies!' They'll expect me to be impressed with their sense of contraceptive responsibility ('Yeah, if you're gonna do it, you gotta to use protection!'), and I'll look stern and say that, yes, I'm impressed. But this is a bluff. I'm perfectly happy for each of the boys to have a few condoms, knowing that they're unlikely to be having sex with anyone except themselves at the moment. I'll make sure not to give them so many condoms, though, that they can afford to go away and blow them up around school, annoying teachers and disrupting lessons.

'Whether or not you're actually in a sexual relationship,' I say to them, 'it's important to practise with a condom, because then, in years ahead, if and when it comes to sex, you'll already be confident with how to put on a condom and with what happens.'

'You mean, you want us to have a poshie!'

'A posh wank, exactly! A wank with a condom…' I check that the girl in the room isn't embarrassed. The boys are also glancing sideways at her, but so far she seems unfazed. 'In the early days of sex,' I go on, 'we tend to rush because – as guys – we're nervous. So we have to learn to slow down. In straight relationships, girls hate it when boys think that sex is all about having an orgasm as quickly as possible and a girl's supposed to lie there and go, "Yeah, that was great," when it wasn't.'

Again I check and she seems okay.

One of the boys says to her, 'Is that what it's like when Luke does it with you, Elsa? Is that what you say to Luke?'

She tells him to fuck off. She tells them all to fuck off.

They shift their embarrassment to one of their own. 'Mikey's never done it before,' one of them says, 'so it's good for him to know about this!'

'How would you know?' Mikey retorts. 'You don't know what I've done!'

'Yeah we do!' says another boy. 'You tried to do it with Sammy Jeffreys, Mikey! Smelly Sammy!'

'No, I didn't,' says Mikey. 'And anyway, Max, you're the one who tried to do it with Sammy Jeffreys and she blew you out!'

They laugh.

'No, Mikey,' says Max. 'She didn't blow me out. She blew me!'

This is all partly for my benefit: the boys establishing their 'lad' credentials. But it's also an expression of their embarrassment and their way of trying to deal with Elsa's presence in the room. When boys are anxious, organizing themselves into a gang is an easy kind of defence. Their jokes usually arise out of their anxieties. I have to stick up for Mikey without seeming to be fighting his battles for him. Condoms may be a useful pretext, but the boys are really here because they want to know about sex. The trouble is that they don't know what to say and can't ask questions for fear of seeming ignorant, especially with a girl in the room. So my job is to anticipate and answer the questions they *would* ask if only they could.

'Girls don't like it when boys boast,' I say, referring back to their teasing of Mikey, 'and they don't like it when boys talk with their mates about things they reckon they've done with girls. Am I right, Elsa?'

She nods, giving nothing away.

'So if you lot go out of here in a few minutes, shouting about how you've got condoms, girls will hear and will think that you can't be trusted to keep things to yourselves when it comes to sex. Or if you come in on Monday morning, telling everyone about what you reckon you've done over the weekend, girls will hear and think "What an idiot!" And you know how annoying it is when girls only want to go out with older guys. But sometimes that's because we get ourselves a bad reputation by acting silly when it comes to sex. And when you've got a reputation, it's really hard to get rid of it. So, with sex, you have to act cool. Keep your business to yourself. Don't go shouting the odds. And don't assume that everyone's straight.'

They look bemused.

Elsa chips in. 'Boys think it's all about getting what they want,' she says. 'Personally, I don't know any of my friends who'd sleep with a boy who had that attitude!'

The boys look at me sheepishly.

'Most boys don't understand,' she goes on. 'And most of them don't know what to do. They think they do, but they don't! And then they say a girl's tight when it's them who doesn't know what to do!'

The boys have gone quiet. Clearly, they have little idea what she's talking about, so I take the opportunity to explain to them about vaginas and lubrication and – again – about the importance of going slowly. They're wearing their Very Serious faces now, keen to know more; in fact, keen to know anything. This is, after all, why they came to the clinic.

'I don't mean to be funny,' says one boy, 'but we were talking in Geography the other day...' He pauses, looking at me, gauging how I'm going to react to whatever it is that he's about to say. 'Well, what we were wondering was...' Again he pauses, half-embarrassed, half-enjoying the limelight. 'Okay, well, we were wondering... Why is it that girls' fannies always smell of fish?'

His friends laugh. They all avoid looking at Elsa.

'That's so stupid!' she says, rounding on them. 'That's so ignorant! And in any case, it's not as bad as cocks that stinks of piss and God knows what else!'

I intervene. We talk about the perils of smegma ('Nob cheese!') and we talk about vaginal discharge. Somehow this leads on to talk of STIs. The boys are worried about what could happen to their genitals if they picked up an infection.

Elsa's a step ahead. 'You shouldn't have to worry, should you, if you're wearing a condom! It's your own fault if you catch something!'

'But condoms split!' says one boy.

'And some of them have holes in them,' says another.

Elsa is wearing her best Aren't-Boys-Useless look. We talk about the unlikelihood of a condom ever splitting or having a hole in it. We go over the technicalities of putting them on correctly. To demonstrate, I get a plastic penis from my bag and immediately the boys start joking about its size. One of them is foolish enough to ask Elsa how this plastic version compares with the real ones she's known.

She tells him that if he could find his own peanut, he'd have achieved something. 'You lot are pathetic!' she says. 'It's got nothing to do with size! It's what you do with it!'

And this, of course, is precisely what the boys know nothing about. They worry about size – of course they do – but they worry more about what to do with it.

'So what *does* turn a girl on then,' one boy asks, 'if it's not a big dick?'

'Wouldn't you like to know!' she replies, knowing full well that the boy really *would* like to know, that he and the other boys are *desperate* to know.

'It's about love,' I interrupt, partly because it's true and partly because I feel obliged to put in a plug for love in the midst of all this mechanical stuff. 'Good sex is loving sex. Being able to talk with your partner. Finding out what your partner likes and doesn't like. It's not about trying to be the big stud or acting like you're in some porn movie. Real life's not like that…'

One boy asks if it's possible to have an eighteen-inch penis because he's seen one on a website. Another boy asks what semen tastes like. Another asks how you can tell if a woman is having an orgasm and another says he's heard that a vagina spurts when a woman has an orgasm.

I look at Elsa but she's keeping quiet, so I answer the questions myself, realizing that the bell's about to go and that I still haven't given the boys their condoms. I ask Elsa if there was anything in particular that she wanted.

'No, I was just bored and came to see what this was all about.'

I tell her that she'll be welcome to visit on her own another time, that there are women working at the clinic as well as men. I ask if she needs condoms.

'No, it's okay,' she says.

Still unclear as to why she chose to come in with the boys, I say that it would be good to see her again and thank her for her help. I give each of the boys two condoms which they quickly shove into their bags, stumbling out of the room together just as the bell is sounding in the distance.

Mikey's lingering behind with something on his mind. 'Can a girl get pregnant if she's never had sex before?' he asks. 'If it's her first time? And if you're wearing a condom?'

'She won't get pregnant if you're wearing the condom properly,' I tell him, 'but of course she could get pregnant if it's her first time. First time or thousandth time, makes no difference!'

He looks at me earnestly. 'What if you're wearing two condoms?'

I don't know whether or not to take this seriously. Has Mikey had sex with someone and worn two condoms?

'One condom is fine,' I say. 'Why do you ask?'

'Oh, nothing,' he says, backing away. 'I was just wondering. Thanks anyway!'

I watch as he hurries down the corridor, trying to catch up with the others, all of them off to a Physics test perhaps, or to another long lesson about images of the supernatural in *Macbeth*.

I see Mikey again a few weeks later. This time I'm waiting in a classroom as he comes in with all the boys in his tutor group: about sixteen of them. Some are silent, others excited and anxious, chatting loudly and asking if we're going to watch porn. Regrettably, it's the one and only sex education lesson they'll have this year; and this year, they've got me as their teacher for an hour and a quarter. During that time, we'll go over many of the things they'll have covered in previous years, but every year their questions will be different: twelve-year-olds ask different questions about condoms from fourteen-year-olds who are more interested in masturbation than sixteen-year-olds.

'I know that you know loads of stuff about sex already,' I say, pandering to their pride, 'and I'm expecting that you'll already know most of the stuff we'll talk about today. But there might be bits and pieces you weren't quite so sure about, because no one knows everything about sex. And if there are things you know that I don't know, it'll be good if you can put your hand up and tell me. It'll also be really good if people feel able to ask questions and say what they're thinking. If I know the answer, I'll tell you, and if I don't, I'll be honest and say so. I'll tell you the technical words as well as the slang words, so you'll hear me say words you don't normally hear members of staff saying. I might say words like penis and masturbation, but I'll also be talking about dicks and wanking.'

Two of the boys in front of me are unable to contain themselves, bursting into hysterics. Some other boys start giggling as well. I let them laugh because they're still settling in and this is just their anxiety talking. Another boy tries to be superior, telling the rest of the group not to be so immature. I see Mikey listening attentively at the back, clearly not one of the more vocal members of the class, amongst whom there'll potentially be gay boys and straight boys, boys who watch lots of porn and boys who never watch porn, boys who've been sexually harmed and boys responsible for harming others: all the boys with their public personas and secret lives.

I explain that the school isn't expecting any of them to be having sex in the near future but that a few of their peers will doubtlessly be starting sexual relationships and, in any case, everyone needs to know about sex. I put in my plug for love and mention the word 'marriage' for the benefit of those parents who'll be asking their sons tonight whether the sex education teacher actually mentioned the word. But unless the boys bring up the subject, we'll say little more about love and little about the quality of relationships. Officially, our session is called Sex and Relationships Education but the boys' anxiety is always to know facts (Luxmoore 2010). Without facts they're vulnerable to teasing and will feel vulnerable going into sexual relationships. In any school, people talk about relationships all the time; teachers are relatively comfortable talking about 'relationships' and the subject comes up in many lessons. Teachers and parents are much less comfortable talking about the facts of sex, about what actually happens. And so, with only one lesson of sex education allocated in the year, it's the facts that we concentrate on.

We start with the perennial issue of penis size. I show them a television clip of flaccid adult penises of slightly varying shapes and sizes. Several boys immediately and ostentatiously shield their eyes while others make pretend-vomit noises. 'This is gross!' says one. 'Do we have to watch this?' asks another, whose real concern, I suspect, is to assure the class that being seen looking at penises doesn't mean that he's gay. I talk to them about circumcision, about wanking (assuring them that they're not the only ones) and about wet dreams, emphasizing the need for privacy and tidiness. 'You don't want your sister running to your mum after you've been locked away in the bathroom and screaming, "Mum! He's been at it again! On the bathroom floor!"' They laugh, beginning to relax. Mikey's smiling too.

I explain female genitalia in detail. None of them have any idea about the exact location of the urethra and most look baffled when we talk about the clitoris. 'Oh, the clit!' announces one boy. 'I've heard it's called the bean,' says another. 'Is it the same as the G-spot?' asks another. We go on to talk about changing fashions in pubic hair and about the crime of female genital mutilation before moving on to condoms. After a quick demonstration and recap, I invite two volunteers to do a challenge. 'I'll give each of you a plastic penis and a condom in its wrapper,' I say as hands are shooting up, trying to attract my attention. 'Your job will be to put the condom onto the penis as quickly as possible,' (more hands), 'except that you'll be blindfolded. In real life, a lot of sex happens in the dark, so it's important to be able to put on a condom when you can't see what you're doing.'

I choose two of the boys who put their hands up first. They move to sit facing the class. I give them the equipment, blindfold them and, encouraging the other boys to stay *really quiet*, say 'Go!'

Immediately one boy can't get the condom out of its wrapper. He struggles with all his might and eventually, panicking because he senses that he's losing the competition, tears into it with his teeth. The other boy has got his condom out of the wrapper and has remembered to squeeze the teat, but is putting the condom on inside out and struggling to roll it down the shaft of the penis. The watching boys are calling out suggestions, completely ignoring my earlier instructions to keep quiet. In frustration, the second boy is now ramming the inside-out condom down the shaft of his plastic penis, while the first boy, desperate to catch up, successfully rolls his condom down the penis but forgets to squeeze the teat and is now trying to rectify his mistake by manoeuvring the fully unrolled condom off the penis and starting all over again.

I call time. We take the blindfolds off and inspect the results. One inside-out condom is stuck halfway down the shaft of a potentially very bruised penis, while the other condom – fully unrolled – is dangling from the end of the penis with the boy – very correctly – still squeezing the teat. We discuss what each of the boys got right and what each of them might have done differently.

Talk of condoms leads to talk of different kinds of condoms, to oral sex, and *that* leads to talk of anal sex. 'Sex up the bum!' one boy explains to the rest. The others have relaxed by now and no one reacts, whereas, years ago, in my experience, there'd have been immediate shouts of 'Benders!', 'Faggots!', 'Bum bandits!' or whatever the local insult happened to be at the time. The boys would have all felt obliged to broadcast their homophobic contempt. Things have moved on, but homophobia is still a blight on the quality of everyday relationships in schools, which is why good, frank, factual sex education is important, helping to demystify sexual practices. In particular, explaining to the boys that one in four straight couples have tried or occasionally or regularly have anal sex has made it clear to the boys I've worked with over the years that anal sex *isn't* the exclusive preserve of gay men, that not all gay men are interested in anal sex anyway, and that any differences in sexual repertoire between gay people and straight people are matters of individual preference rather than tribal loyalty.

Throughout all this, Mikey remains attentive, letting the more vocal members of the class have their say. We're running out of time. I ask for one last question but no one seems to have one. The boys look at each other, keen for someone to ask something. One boy puts up his hand as the bell goes. 'Yeah,' he says, grinning. 'I've got a question… Why do girls' fannies always smell of fish?'

As they go out of the classroom, I call after Mikey. I'm still curious about his question at the end of the lunchtime clinic three weeks ago. 'How was the lesson today?' I ask him. 'Did you learn anything?'

'A bit,' he says, 'but nothing I didn't know already.'

I nod approvingly. 'And you know the other guys in the class, Mikey… Do you think it was about right for them? Anything you think I could have done differently?'

'Not really,' he says. 'It was okay.'

As casually as possible, I ask, 'Are you in a relationship yourself at the moment?'

He nods.

'Anyone I know? Anyone at school?'

'You don't know her.'

'Is she from round here?'

'Not really. She lives in Germany. Her dad's in the army.'

'Do you see her much?'

'We were going to meet up last summer,' he explains, 'but she had to go on holiday with her family. So we might be going to meet this summer.'

It begins to dawn on me. 'Have you met her face-to-face yet?'

'Not yet,' he says, 'but we talk every night.'

'And she's nice?'

'Yeah, she's really nice.'

He leaves and I'm reminded that young people approach relationships in so many different ways. Some will strut their stuff, boasting and bragging like the boys at the clinic. Some will embark on sexual relationships at the earliest possible opportunity, telling the whole world about their experiences. Others, like Mikey, will be cautious, shy, secretive, unconfident, sometimes muddled about the practicalities of sex (I think of Mikey's two condoms question) but driven just as powerfully by the need to love and be loved.

Later that day, a member of staff contacts me to ask if I have any counselling vacancies and whether I might be able to see a fifteen-year-old girl who took an overdose at the weekend.

'Nothing terrible,' says my colleague, 'but clearly something's going on and the doctor's asked if she can see a counsellor in school. And I've just had her mum on the phone, who's obviously concerned because so far they've got nowhere with talking to her at home. And to be honest with you, I've noticed that she hasn't seemed to be herself around school lately.'

I ask for the girl's name.

'I think you might know her? I saw her earlier today and she mentioned that she knew you. Elsa Lloyd?'

Elsa! Perhaps her visit to the lunchtime clinic was an opportunity to check me out, as if she was sensing that she needed help, though not with anything as mundane as contraception. At the time I remember being pleased that we'd got on well in the room with the five boys. I'd liked her.

A few days later, I meet with a girl who, on her own, is much more reserved and serious than the feisty, sweary girl who held her own so effectively with the boys.

'I didn't take a lot,' she says. 'Only about twelve tablets but I *did* want to die. Or I did at the time … I don't know really.'

Apparently her mother realized that something was wrong when Elsa came downstairs, fell over and couldn't get up again. Her mother called the ambulance but still with no idea as to what might be wrong. 'She thought I might have meningitis! I was completely out of it. And I'd had a bit to drink as well. But it wasn't till I was in the ambulance that they realized what I'd done. Well, they asked, and so I told them. And then Mum got all upset and they were all talking about it in the hospital, but I didn't really tell them anything else, so when I got home, they made me go and see the doctor and he said to come and see you.'

She pauses, looking up, as if expecting me now to prescribe something. I suggest that we start at the beginning.

'Everything was all right until a month ago. I didn't have any problems. Well, apart from my dad. We've never got on. But my boyfriend, Luke, he was really pissing me off. I knew he was talking to other girls but he wouldn't admit it. And then he said we should go on a break and I knew it was because he'd been seeing this girl. And, I don't know… I just sort of lost it and told him I never wanted to see him again. And then he called me a slut, and that was it really!'

'A slut?'

'Yeah, he actually used that word.'

I ask if her relationship with Luke had been sexual because, even if the answer's no, at least we'll have established sex as one of the things we can talk about if Elsa chooses.

'Yeah, it was sexual, but nothing to write home about, if you know what I mean. Just sex, really.'

I ask what she loved and perhaps still loves about Luke.

'Nothing! He's a twat! I hate him! When he found out about the tablets he was all babe-this and babe-that, like he cared. But I knew he didn't really.'

I ask if she's still seeing him.

'I am, but I don't know why. I must be a complete idiot!'

'Presumably there are things about him that you still like…?'

She shrugs. 'He can be nice if he wants to be. It'd be all right if he was like that all the time…' She pauses. 'Him and my dad have never got on. My dad hates him!' She describes her life at home where her parents argue all the time, apparently, with her father taking his frustrations out on Elsa, accusing her of lying, disobedience, laziness, promiscuity: all the things fathers traditionally condemn in daughters who are growing up and who no longer need Daddy for wisdom and protection.

I begin to wonder about Luke's usefulness as a way of fighting her father, as a way of telling her father that she no longer needs someone to control her life; that nowadays she can make her own choices about boys, boys who represent all the things that she knows make her father angry. I wonder whether her overdose was less about Luke and more about her relationships at home. I remember my colleague saying that Elsa hadn't seemed to be herself lately and wonder whether that's the real issue: 'Who am I? If I'm no longer my father's little girl and don't want to be his little girl, then who am I? Have I become a lying, disobedient, lazy, promiscuous girl like my father says? A slut? Am I the feisty, confident girl who holds her own in a room full of boys, or am I the reserved, serious girl who comes for counselling?'

She tells me more about her father, about how their relationship has changed over the years, about how hurtful his criticisms have been, about meeting Luke and thinking that he was The Best until she discovered that he wasn't. She tells me about trying to do well at school and keep her friends; about wondering whether anyone really loves anyone else or whether everyone's pretending. She tells me about feeling alone sometimes, really alone, as if no one cares about her or even thinks about her.

'When it happened, there was no one I could tell.'

'When you took the tablets?'

'No, before that.'

'No one you could tell about what, Elsa?'

She looks away. 'Promise you won't say anything to anyone?'

I tell her I can't promise that.

'Oh well,' she says, looking weary, 'I suppose you might as well know... The real reason I took the tablets was because I thought I was pregnant. Well, I *was* pregnant...'

She waits for my reaction.

'...but it's all right now, I'm not pregnant.'

'Because you had an abortion?'

'No, because I did another test when I got home from the hospital and it turns out I'm not pregnant. And I'm on my period now so I can't be. But the first test I did, it said I was pregnant.'

'And that was before you took the tablets?'

'I told Luke about it and he didn't want to know. He said it was my fault for not remembering the pill. And he actually asked me if the baby was his! I mean, he *actually* asked!' Her eyes fill with tears. 'So after that I couldn't tell anyone, because I knew exactly what my dad would say! And I didn't want to tell my mum in case she told my dad!'

'You were on your own, Elsa...'

'I didn't know what to do. I felt like I might as well be dead. So I thought, what the fuck!'

'And had a drink and took the tablets...'

'I regret it now,' she says. 'Now it turns out I'm not pregnant. But at the time I didn't know what to do...'

I try to imagine how afraid a fifteen-year-old person might have felt, believing herself to be pregnant, that everything was suddenly out of her control and that all her father's words had apparently come true: 'You're a slut, Elsa! A slut!' I try to imagine how alone she might have felt, unable to go backwards and afraid to go forwards. Not knowing what to do. Hating herself. Waiting to be found out... I imagine that being dead might very well have seemed like the best option at the time.

She allows me to arrange an appointment for her with the sexual health nurse at the clinic the following lunchtime, so that she can be absolutely clear what it was that happened with the pregnancy and can check that her contraceptive pill is still appropriate.

I wonder about telling her parents what I know... Elsa's fifteen and having consensual sex with her sixteen-year-old boyfriend. She's responsible enough to have got herself on the pill, but then she thought she might be pregnant, imagined her parents' reaction and took an overdose. Her parents found out about the overdose, so they already know that something's the matter with their daughter, even if they don't know the whole story. They know that she's seeing me. She's probably no longer pregnant, is in no obvious danger at the moment and is going to meet with the nurse tomorrow. I'll check that she keeps that appointment...

I wonder what it would do to Elsa if I told her parents? Would she ever trust me again? Would telling her parents feel like someone was looking after her best interests or would it feel like another person betraying her? Would she then refuse to see me and refuse to see the nurse as well? Would she effectively give up on herself? I think about the consequences of *not* telling her parents. They'd be upset if they found out. They might be angry with me...

I'm sure that the nurse will keep whatever Elsa says confidential. Under the circumstances I decide that I won't contact her parents.

'It would be great if you could talk to your mum,' I suggest. 'I could talk to her for you if you wanted. Or we could do it together.'

She looks at me as if I've just suggested that we dance naked together in the canteen at breaktime.

'Okay, Elsa, okay! But you and I need to keep meeting, because there's a lot to talk about.'

'Promise you won't tell my parents?'

I repeat that I can't make that promise, but that if I did need to speak to her parents at some point in the future, I wouldn't do it behind her back. 'It sounds like it's been a really horrible time for you, Elsa. Like the scariest, loneliest time. And the saddest.'

The tears trickle down her cheeks. She dabs the corners of her eyes with a tissue, trying to stop her make-up from running.

'I think you've done bloody well, Elsa, to have got this far. To have survived. To be dealing with it all...'

'I haven't dealt with anything though, have I,' she says. 'I'm just some stupid bitch who took an overdose! I'm just a drama queen! That's what they'll all be saying!'

It's as if she has well and truly internalized the harshness of her father's voice. I tell her it's not true. 'You're not a stupid bitch and you're not a drama queen. You're a person who had a horrible shock and then found out that her boyfriend wouldn't stick up for her. You're a person who felt alone and didn't know what to do. Who felt unloved. Who felt that people would despise her. And you're a person who tends to blame herself anyway! But you're also a person who can be very responsible, who tries her best, who loves people and hates it when they let her down. You're a person who takes her life seriously, Elsa. Good for you! *And*, as I happen to know from our conversation with those boys a few weeks ago, you're also a person who's good at sticking up for herself and who has an excellent sense of humour. You're *lots* of things, Elsa!'

She smiles through her tears. 'Not all bad, then?'

'No, not all bad!'

In the weeks ahead we'll explore all these parts of Elsa in more detail. But for now it's enough to acknowledge that they *all* exist, that she makes sense, that she's not going mad.

Our session ends and she gets up to go, calmer now. I ask whether she ever sees any of the boys from the lunchtime clinic.

'Not really,' she says, smiling, 'but they're all right most of the time, that lot. They don't bother me. They were just being annoying that day. They get like that sometimes!'

4

MY BODY, MY SELF

GETTING OUT OF bed in the morning and going to a school that expresses or represses sexuality, working out what exactly goes on in sexual relationships, developing sexual feelings about other people... In the midst of all this, young people are getting used to their own bodies, bodies that keep changing.

'I hate the way I look!' says Sheron, glaring, as if to warn me that any sensible person would be very unwise to challenge her on this.

I ask what it is that she hates.

'Everything! My hair! My nose! My stupid eyebrows! I hate everything!'

I say that if that's her truth and if she's sticking to it, then I'm not going to contradict her. 'You'll have your reasons for hating the way you look, Sheron, whatever anyone else might say.'

'No, other people say it as well!' she says, softening. 'They say I look like a man. They ask me if I've got a penis.'

I'm reminded of how cruel young people can be. Sheron's fourteen and tall for her age. She looks fine to me. I imagine that people would say that she's 'big boned' or 'statuesque', meaning that she isn't the stereotypically cute, slender coquette whom boys her age tend to like. No doubt they call her 'butch' because she's tall, or 'manly' because her jaw's a bit square and doesn't taper neatly like a film star's.

The way we think about our bodies is, to some extent, socially conditioned (Nitsun 2006). In some cultures, fat is bad and thin is good; while in others, fat is good and thin is bad. Certainly, the way a girl looks to other people will be one of the things affecting the way she feels about herself. It'll affect the way she dresses: perhaps a baggy jumper to hide her breasts, make-up to look more exotic, a short skirt if she feels confident about her legs, trousers if she doesn't... Sheron tells me that she hates her hair, nose and eyebrows. What she doesn't say is 'I hate my breasts! I hate my belly! I hate my bum!' yet those may well be parts of her body about which she's more concerned. She'd probably disagree with Freud (1905) and Lacan (1958) that her lack of a penis leaves her feeling depleted ('Why would I want a dick?'), but she might well agree with Ensler (2001) in adding 'my vagina' to the list of things that she and other girls are conditioned to dislike about themselves. Her hair, nose and eyebrows are the socially acceptable objects of her disgust, the things she can tell me about. She'd never say to me, 'I hate my breasts! I hate them being so small... Or so big... Or lopsided... Or flat... Or pointy...'

There are plenty of young people for whom the real issue provoking their shyness or anger is that they feel bad about the way they look. It's hard to talk about this. Young people know perfectly well the terrible, unfair truth that the way they look will have a bearing on their future lives. 'With puberty, the future not only approaches: it takes residence in her body...', writes De Beauvoir (1949, p.351) in her famous study. Young people have no control over the way their bodies change and grow. They can spend hours agonizing in front of a mirror, but it makes no difference. De Beauvoir goes on, '…the lie to which an adolescent girl is condemned is that she must pretend to be an object, and a fascinating one, when she senses herself as an uncertain, dissociated being, well aware of her blemishes' (p.380).

In principle, Sheron's no worse off than a girl of the same age who feels cursed with a curvaceous body and film star face: cursed because, for years to come, this girl must withstand the advances and assumptions of boys and men; cursed by conventional beauty in the way that Sheron feels cursed by her unconventional beauty. Sheron wants to punch the people who say that she looks like a man, and of course her parents tell her to ignore such stupid people. 'But people never stop saying it,' she says. 'They go on about it all the time. They've been saying it since I was in primary school! Mostly, I try and get on with my life, but sometimes they get to me.'

I ask about her life, knowing that we can come back to her feelings about her body in due course. She talks about her family and somehow we get onto the subject of her uncle who left his wife and went off with his wife's best friend. Sheron's outraged. She says that she can't forgive her uncle. She can't stand to be in the same room as him.

We talk about why affairs happen and who's to blame. I say that it's hard when we're attracted to people we shouldn't be attracted to.

'He shouldn't have left her, though!' says Sheron. 'Not when they'd been together for ten years! He could have told Angie he liked the other woman. And then they could have talked about it and sorted it out and maybe they could have stayed together.' Apparently her uncle left without warning. 'Just like that. And now he's living with his girlfriend and Angie's on her own with no one for her.'

I wonder to myself how much Sheron sees herself in the story of the betrayed wife, no longer attractive to her husband and abandoned without warning. Indeed, I wonder how much Sheron feels betrayed by *life*, no longer a little girl but obliged to become tall with a square jaw, teased because of how she looks and worrying that there'll be no one in the world to love her. And all because of the way she looks.

'He's an ugly pig!' she rants. 'His girlfriend'll soon get tired of him once she realizes what a bastard he is! And then he'll realize it was a mistake leaving Angie. But by then it'll be too late!'

I ask how her aunt has been since the split.

'Not good! You can see how upset she is. She pretends she isn't, but she is, really.'

Just like you, Sheron, I think to myself: pretending not to care but caring a lot. She and her aunt don't get time alone to talk. I ask Sheron what she'd say to Angie if she had the opportunity.

'I'd tell her she's better off without him and that she'll find someone better.'

'And if she was to lose confidence in herself? If she was to start thinking that no one would ever fancy her again?'

'I'd tell her not to worry. Angie's got a great personality. And she's really pretty.'

'Like you, Sheron?'

'No, not like me at all! I'm not pretty!'

I curse myself for trying to make an overt connection between Sheron and her aunt. A girl's view of herself is never changed by one rather lame therapeutic manoeuvre. In suggesting to Sheron that she might take her own advice, my need to rescue her from hating herself got the better of me, whereas *her* need was probably to have her hatred of her body and her fear of the future acknowledged, to be allowed to be afraid of these things *with* someone rather than on her own.

Media images of 'perfect' bodies are often blamed for young people's dissatisfaction with their bodies. These images and the commodification of women's bodies certainly don't help, but I imagine that for centuries young people have compared their bodies with those of their heroes and heroines. Worrying about one's appearance isn't a modern phenomenon. Feeling happy or unhappy about one's appearance begins much earlier in life.

To begin with, a baby doesn't experience itself as anything other than a body desperately needing to attach in order to be safe. The baby internalizes a sense of its body as either desirable and beautiful or loathsome and ugly from the messages it receives from care-givers (Stern 1985). These messages will be verbal (words and sounds accompanied by smiles of delight or frowns of displeasure) but the baby will also receive messages from the way in which it's handled: with confidence and relish or with anxiety and resentment. A baby internalizes the attitude of other people to its body (Schwartz 2007). In other words, 'How I feel about myself will depend on the messages I receive about my body from the people around me.'

Any subjective sense of 'me' as distinct from 'my body' comes later, comes gradually. If we begin with a sense of ourselves as attractive or unattractive bodies, then before long we find ourselves doing things that are no longer merely physical and yet seem to interest people (Stern 1985). We start communicating in other ways; we start to have moods;

we start to play and joke with the people around us. In short, we start to exist as personalities. Our bodies are no longer the sum of who we are. Though always connected, 'me' and 'my body' are no longer quite the same thing. We've become interesting as personalities because now we have ideas, we can initiate, we're able to understand and respond to other people's moods.

But all this takes developmental time. As teenagers, most young people are still wrestling with the distinction between 'me' and 'my body'. They're still worrying, 'If I was thinner, would people love me more? If I dyed my hair or got a tattoo, would that make up for the way I look? To what extent is my inner sense of worth determined by my body's outward appearance?' Saying to a young person like Sheron that 'It's who you are inside that matters!' may well be true but, as a plea, often falls on deaf ears when the relationship between 'who I am on the inside' and 'who I am on the outside' is so close.

Still cursing myself for trying to rescue Sheron in such a clumsy manner, I resolve to be a thoughtful and patient counsellor rather than a cheery coach or well-meaning friend. Her self-confidence doesn't depend on me. Over the next few years, other experiences will affect the way she sees herself. Smaller girls will grow taller. Some will grow to be as tall as Sheron. She'll get better at dressing to impress. She'll begin to have friends who are boys. When she's sixteen, she and her friends will probably decide to go to the leaving-school Ball, confident enough now to take that risk.

For young people, The Ball marks an uncomfortable coming-together of friendship and sexuality. There are girls who'll admit to having planned their ball dress for years and others who'll say that they've never given it a moment's thought. Some will describe their dresses in proud detail, getting their phones out to show me the pictures. Others will be more circumspect, saying that they'll probably find something to wear at the last minute.

Hearing about the dress, I'll say that it sounds great. Seeing pictures of it, I'll say that it looks wonderful, because to say anything else would be unkind. Year after year, I'm impressed that so many girls find the confidence to go through this rite of passage: dressing up in expensive clothes for the parental cameras, for the approval of friends, for boys to stare and fantasize. I sometimes wonder how much a ball dress is effectively a rehearsal for a wedding dress. But at the same time, I sympathize with the girls who refuse to take part in any of this, unwilling to compete with all the glitter and hair-curling or simply feeling that it's demeaning still to be judged as a body after so many years of feminist progress.

Until the day she leaves school, Sheron and I will continue to talk about the loyalties and betrayals of her life, the ups and downs of growing up, where bodies change of their own accord and where there's nothing that Sheron can do but try to forgive and accept the one she's got with all its beauties and imperfections. She's not unusual. So many young people are dissatisfied with their bodies: bodies over which they have no control, bodies genetically inherited from their 'stupid' parents, bodies seeping blood and semen, snot and piss. As Sheron knows, critical comments about the way a body looks feel personal ('Like they were talking about me!') because talking about someone's body can feel like talking about the person inside the body. Young people are forever interested in ways of getting thinner, larger, sexier, more attractive in the belief that, if only they could perfect their bodies, they'd perfect themselves. They smear on make-up; they fantasize about cosmetic surgery; they punish their bodies with self-harm or attempt to shape their bodies through diet and exercise, through lifting weights. When adults say to a young person like Sheron, 'You're fine as you are! We love you for who you are, not for what you look like! It's your personality that matters!', they're trying to be helpful, but that helpfulness usually falls on deaf ears. 'Yes,' thinks the young person, 'that's all very well for you to say – you're not the one who looks like this!' I think it's more helpful to understand why a young person's body feels so important, and why the distinction between 'me' and 'my body' feels so hard to make. Rather than offering cheap reassurances, it's more helpful to acknowledge and bear with young people the anxieties and frustrations of living with a body that, like it or not, will inevitably be seen and judged by other people.

Unable to bear these anxieties and frustrations, some young people stay in their rooms, refusing to be seen by anyone. Jazmin says she can't bear it when people see her eating. She also gets nervous about being seen shopping or waiting for the bus. 'I wasn't like it before,' she says. 'I don't know why I've got like this. I don't even like going to parties now, which makes it really difficult because I have to make up excuses to tell my friends, and then they think I'm being anti-social…'

Being seen is a primitive experience. As babies, we must attract attention to ourselves or die, and as a fifteen-year-old girl, Jazmin must find ways of being seen in the world in order to live normally. Yet being seen will mean being judged. She may well hate being seen eating, shopping and catching the bus. Other young people would add to that list their hatred of being seen reading aloud in class, seen without make-up, seen without friends, seen trampolining or in a swimming costume... The list would go on. The anxieties are endless. Fights erupt sometimes when one person is accused of looking at another and the look is interpreted as hostile, scornful or humiliating. 'What you looking at? You looking at me?' For some young people, phobias develop as ways of desperately trying to control these situations. Jazmin stays in her room where no one can see her and where she hopes to remain in control.

I know that counsellors shouldn't jump to conclusions but I can't help myself. On hearing her story, my first guess is that the reason why she hates being seen is because she feels ugly inside, full of hatred, and fears that if people see her, they'll see that ugliness. Gilligan (2000) suggests that shame always drives our need to stay hidden. My second guess is that she's afraid of being seen sexually: of people seeing the outline of her breasts and bum. My third guess is that she's afraid of being seen eating because of some anxiety about bodily waste, about orifices, about mess and all the things that go into and come out of us.

I sit with her, wondering how to test these hypotheses. But I'm missing the most obvious thing: Jazmin has terrible spots all over her forehead, all over cheeks and chin. In fact, she has more spots than most young people ever have to endure, and I wonder whether this is the elephant in the room: whether Jazmin hates being seen because she hates people seeing her scabby spots roughly covered over with heavy foundation.

I find a way of saying something about 'the way we look' and suddenly she's off, telling me about what it's like to have spots, about how much they blight her life, affecting everything. She tells me that she's tried all sorts of treatments and *still* nothing works; that there's nothing she can do except wait to grow older, but that this might take years with people pretending not to notice, with no one liking her or wanting to kiss her, with wanting to retreat from social situations to avoid the embarrassment of having such terrible spots.

She goes to school. She smiles. She does her best. I'm touched by the courage of a girl who doesn't deserve any of this: a kind, friendly girl living with the brutal unfairness of spots at a time in her life when she probably longs to look glamorous and beautiful. I want to reassure her ('They'll get better! It's who you are inside that counts!'), but I know that other people will have offered the same reassurances. They'll have made no difference. Instead, I must bear my inability to help her, just as she must bear her wretched spots. But if together we can acknowledge and talk about the spots, then, at least in counselling, she can be seen and can perhaps begin to feel more confident. She can risk becoming visible in the counselling room rather than remaining determinedly, unhappily invisible in her room at home.

It's as if Jazmin's whole identity at the moment is bound up with her spots. Thinking about the relationship between our minds and bodies, Winnicott (1975) describes the mind developing a 'false localisation' whereby a person's whole sense of identity becomes located in a part of the body. Jazmin feels that she *is* her spots. There are boys whose identity is bound up with being physically small for their age (Luxmoore 2006). There are other boys about whom girls complain, 'He does his talking with his fists!' or 'He thinks with his dick!'; boys whose sense of themselves is reduced to a single physical characteristic. This split between mind and body (psyche and soma) occurs originally in relation to an 'environmental mother', argues Winnicott in the same paper. A baby might be developing nicely, learning to think about itself as *simultaneously* a mind and a body, the one inseparable from the other. But then things happen unexpectedly, something goes wrong and the 'environmental mother' (the people around) can't cope. The baby feels anxious, afraid, and reverts to being merely a body again, abandoning thought, abandoning any concern for other people, intent only on staying safe and trying to survive physically at all costs.

There are babies who become children and appear never to move beyond a purely physical sense of themselves. They get stuck developmentally, growing older and bigger yet without learning to think of themselves as more than a body. For them, physical gratification is all that matters. With no experience of an environmental mother mirroring them back to themselves, taking an interest in them as thinking, feeling beings, they develop no interest in anyone else. Eventually they grow into young people, stuck with a sense that bodily survival and triumph are the only things that matter. They're 'all front', with no internal, subjective life that they can talk about, their feelings split off and quashed as too unsettling, too disruptive, too strange to contemplate.

I know nothing about what Tray's life was like when he was a baby but meet an intelligent seventeen-year-old exhibiting this same developmental stuckness.

'I've come because I'm worried about my exams,' he explains. 'I'm not sleeping and my mum suggested I should come and see you.' His ambition is to run a famous firm of accountants, he tells me, making lots of money and being admired as a powerful man, ruthlessly dispatching workers who don't live up to his standards.

'They'll admire you, Tray,' I say to him, 'but they probably won't love you ...'

'What d'you mean?'

'Being successful and being loved aren't necessarily the same thing. People might admire your ruthlessness; they might want to be friends with you because you'll have lots of money. But that doesn't mean that they'll love you.'

He genuinely doesn't understand.

'They'll love you for your vulnerability. For your kindness. They'll love you for your failures. And for the times when you forgive them their failures.' I keep explaining but he has no idea what I'm talking about.

One day I ask, as matter-of-factly as possible, 'How's your love life, Tray?'

'What d'you mean?'

'Are you single? Have you got people wanting to go out with you?'

He blushes. 'Shouldn't think so!'

'Do you fancy anyone?'

On the one hand, I have to avoid shaming him because there's absolutely no reason why he *should* fancy anyone. But on the other hand, I have to float the possibility that he might fancy someone, if only to bring sexuality overtly into our conversation as a part of Tray that's interesting. As a rule, I ask lots of questions about what he *feels* and, as a rule, he answers by telling me what he *does*. I wonder about his relationship with his body and its physical sensations. Does he experience his body as just a nuisance, a problem to be overcome through ascetic disregard? To be dismissed like an employee who doesn't fit the corporate image? How does Tray experience food and drink? Handshakes? Bathing? Orgasm?

I ask how members of his family express affection.

'We have debates.'

'Debates?'

'Yeah, about politics and things like that.'

'What if someone wants to show how much they care about someone else?'

He explains to me that, in his family, they don't do that.

'Do people ever hug each other?'

'Not really,' he says. 'My mum tries to do that to me sometimes but she knows I don't like it.'

'Because...?'

'I don't know. It's not necessary. It feels weird.'

'Weird because it's hard to know how to respond?'

'Yeah!'

I agree with him that sometimes it takes a while to get used to being hugged. 'You and I might like each other, Tray, but we probably wouldn't hug each other.'

'Exactly!'

'So I wonder how we would know what we feel about each other?'

He looks at me, as if expecting to be told the answer. Rarely do I talk with young people about our here-and-now relationship in the counselling room because that conversation is usually too exposing, too embarrassing for young people and the power relationship between us too unequal (Luxmoore 2014). But with Tray I decide that we can treat our relationship as a chance to practise feeling something and then trying to describe that feeling.

'I feel close to you, Tray, when I sense that you're afraid and don't know what to do about something.'

He thanks me.

'Can you say more about the times when you do feel afraid?'

He looks puzzled. 'I tell myself all the reasons why it's stupid being afraid.'

'What's the afraid feeling like?'

'I don't like it.'

His parents may be wonderful people, but presumably at some point in his life Tray believed himself to be in danger and the fear set in. His scared feelings threatened his survival and had to be dealt with. Theoretically, he turned himself into a chief accountant, a managing director ruthlessly dispatching other people the way he'd learned to dispatch his own feelings. It may well be that, as a baby or child, there were specific occasions when Tray felt unnerved and alone, and it may be that we'll revisit some of these experiences in our conversations, detoxifying and taking away some of their power, freeing him to become more confident in acknowledging his feelings, feelings that brought him to me in the first place, worrying about his exams and unable to sleep. But it'll take time.

Just as Tray splits his thoughts from his feelings, so there are boys who effectively split the physical, sexual part of themselves from their private, internal identities; boys who end up thinking with their dicks (as girls might say); boys who talk about and treat girls as sexualized objects; boys who can cope with a 'shag' or a 'fuck' but not with a relationship.

'They're pathetic!' says Sami. 'All they do is show off and talk about sex. And everyone knows they haven't done anything! They've got a really bad attitude. Some of them try and touch you when teachers aren't looking. They're so annoying!'

She's talking about the boys she comes into contact with at school, but fourteen-year-old Sami could be ten years older and talking about men in a bar, men she might be interested in knowing but whose behaviour fills her with contempt.

'They reckon it's all about sex! They act like it's all they're interested in, but everyone knows that's not what they're like really. Well, most of them.'

I ask if she has boys who like her.

'Not really,' she says. 'And I wouldn't want to go out with any of them anyway. I've got one friend who's a boy. Lenny. He comes round with us a lot. He's not like the other boys. He doesn't try and show off all the time!'

There are many kinds of boys, but most girls describe only two kinds: the leering, loud-mouthed boy who's always making jokes about sex, and the shy, feminine boy who becomes an honorary member of the girls' gang, allowed to join in the girls' conversations and share some of their secrets.

'Lenny's okay. If the other boys were more like him it would be okay,' says Sami. 'I'd never go out with him, though. Don't get me wrong – I really like him. He's just not that kind of boy.'

'Because?'

'I don't know! He just isn't.'

I suspect that Lenny's passivity is what makes him so attractive as a friend but stops him being boyfriend material. I suspect that Sami would rather go out with one of the louder boys, if only…

'If only they didn't act so pathetically!' she says. 'Calling us lesbians all the time! If only they could talk normally without everything having to be about sex!'

Before long, one of her friends will typically break ranks and go out with one of The Pathetic Boys, much to the dismay of Sami and her friends. 'Should be chicks before dicks!' they'll complain to the traitorous girl. The event will beg questions for the rest of them. 'To what extent are we just bodies boys want for sex, and to what extent can we hope for more, for better? For conversation and closeness? For support and trust? For fun that doesn't have to end in sex? And what about our own sexual needs? To what extent will we ever be able to trust boys to be sensitive and kind, understanding sex as a two-way thing rather than as a competitive dash to the finish?' Using Freud's language, Welldon (1988) argues that girls are grounded in the reality principle, whereas boys 'are more prone to the pleasure principle' (p.21) because they're not the ones who'll become pregnant and be expected to look after the child.

Straight, gay or bisexual, most young people spend their teenage years muddling through, learning from their mistakes. Only a few survive unscathed, sometimes negotiating their relationships with astonishing skill.

'Take Brendan,' says Sami.

'Brendan?'

'Brendan Rodriguez? In the year above? I was supposed to be going out with him earlier this year, but he cheated on me and the first I knew about it was from one of his friends! He went with a girl in the year above and, when I asked him why he did it, he said he didn't know! He said they were at a party and he was drunk and it just happened.'

I ask if Brendan had sex with the girl.

Sami doesn't know. 'But probably,' she says scornfully, 'if that's what he wanted and if he knew he could get it from her.'

I ask if her own relationship with Brendan had been a sexual one.

'Not really,' she says. 'I mean, we did things, you know, but not full-on sex if that's what you mean.'

'And you think that's what Brendan was really interested in?'

'I don't know,' she says, worrying. 'I mean, I thought we were getting on okay. He knew I wanted to wait and he said he was fine about that. But then he goes and does it with some stupid bitch he barely knows!'

Sexual jealousy and shame are potent. They leave Sami and her friends wondering 'What's normal? What do I want? When he says he wants to have sex with me because he loves me, what should I think? Or when he says he wants us to wait, should I believe him?' Sami wrestles with these questions overtly but, in my experience, all girls – lesbian, straight, bisexual – live with the same questions. Some can talk with a parent but many can't, especially if the conversation involves coming out as lesbian or bisexual. Young people live in silent uncertainty and sometimes that uncertainty is too much: it gets acted out at their own or at other people's expense, as young people reach for tangible proof, for answers, for an end to the terrible uncertainty (Luxmoore 2010). Sami's fluctuating attitudes towards schoolwork, for example, become expressions of her attempts to resolve other, underlying sexual uncertainties. There are times when she gives up on schoolwork altogether, believing that everything is out of her control and that there's no point trying. At other times, she resolves to work hard at school, believing that the future is in her hands, that good things are possible. Sometimes a bad mark feels like a betrayal when she's put in a lot of effort. At other times she loses interest when a lesson that promised so much turns out not to be as interesting as she hoped. Just like a boy.

All young people wrestle with their sense of agency, with the extent to which they can control the world or are controlled by it. But sexual and romantic agency ('Is she attracted to me? Do I love her? What can I do about the situation?') is especially hard to gauge and talk about without reverting to a child's sense of being a body and no more, a body choosing simply to have sex or not to have sex.

'I reckon I'd be better off on my own,' says Sami, 'then I won't have to deal with stupid, pathetic boys. Or maybe I'll become a lesbian! At least they don't cheat on each other!'

She sees my eyebrows raised.

'Okay! Maybe I'll become a nun!'

'Do nuns ever feel betrayed?'

'Okay, okay!' she laughs. 'Forget that! Maybe I'll just have sex with loads of boys and cheat on them all, so they know what it's like!'

Sami's imagined revenge would be to treat boys merely as bodies. Nussbaum (2001) describes the difficulty philosophers have always had in trying not to separate physical sex from emotional love but in allowing for 'sexual love' or 'erotic love' as the integration of bodily desire and emotional longing. Sixteen-year-old Mitchell is therefore in an age-old tradition of people trying to understand their bodies in relation to their hearts and minds.

He's been coming to see me for well over a year and, recently, he's been feeling great. He's fallen in love with Jack and – lo and behold – Jack loves Mitchell! Everything in Mitchell's life suddenly seems bearable: the emotional abuse at home, the bullying at school, the loneliness and aggravation… None of these things seems to matter any more because now he loves Jack and Jack loves him. Perfect! There's only one problem…

'He doesn't want to do it as much as I do!'

Mitchell's constant desire for sex with his boyfriend is partly a matter of happy lust and partly a matter of keeping the past at bay, reassuring himself that he really is loveable. 'When it comes to sexuality,' writes Phillips (2010), 'excess is the sign of the fear of scarcity' (p.22). So when Jack's tired or distracted or just doesn't feel like sex, Mitchell worries that this is the beginning of the end of their relationship. His confidence is disturbed on these occasions in ways that Jack probably doesn't understand.

He asks if he can bring Jack to meet me so that we can discuss it together, and a week later, he sits there coyly, looking at Jack, looking at me, looking back at Jack. 'Shall I say?'

Jack nods.

'Well, it's about sex,' says Mitchell, checking with Jack again, 'isn't it?'

Jack keeps quiet. I feel sorry for him. As a favour, he's agreed to meet with Mitchell's counsellor, someone he's never met before. I'm impressed.

'The problem is that I like doing it more than he does,' says Mitchell before correcting himself. 'Well, no, you *do* like doing it, but sometimes you don't.'

I ask Jack what he'd like to say to Mitchell.

'I've told you I just don't want to do it the whole time, that's all.'

'See!' says Mitchell. 'And then I think he doesn't love me any more. And then we have arguments. But it's normal to want sex when you're young, isn't it?'

I say something bland about sexual relationships taking time to settle down as people get to know each other and that most people worry about whether they have sex too often or not often enough. I'm reminded of Phillips's (2005) remark that 'Simply because we have been children our sexuality is going to be an uneasy mix of the imperious and the servile' (p.125). All young people are learning to regulate their appetites. I imagine Mitchell, imperious and demanding at times and, at other times, servile and begging.

'But what if he *never* wants to do it as much as I do?'

Jack squirms with embarrassment.

'Jack can do whatever he wants,' I say to Mitchell. 'If he doesn't want to have sex as often as you do, that doesn't mean he doesn't love you.'

Jack's pleased. 'That's exactly what I said!'

Clearly, Mitchell isn't getting the answer he was hoping for. 'So how am I supposed to know if he loves me?'

'Because I tell you!' says Jack, looking straight at him. 'I tell you every day!'

'But you've told other people you love them!' replies Mitchell, getting in a sly dig. 'You've said it to all the other people you've been out with!'

'You're both right,' I say, intervening. 'Jack can't do any more than tell you what he feels, Mitchell. He can't *prove* anything. He can only tell you the truth the way he sees it. And you have a right to be cautious about believing him. You've been hurt before in your life when people have broken their promises, so of course you don't want to be hurt again. And having sex might be great but it doesn't necessarily prove anything. You could both be horny and having sex together ten times a day...'

They laugh.

'That wouldn't mean that you were always going to be in love with each other! Sex might be only *one* of the ways in which Jack loves you, Mitchell.'

Eventually they leave in reasonable humour, though with Mitchell still agitating. The next time he and I meet (without Jack), we work hard on his need to repair the past through sex, his need for sex as proof of love. We think about the long journey that he and Jack have begun to see whether their relationship endures, with or without lots of sex. Freud (1912) famously observes that men tend to separate love and desire, seeing women as either madonnas or whores: 'Where such men love they have no desire and where they desire they can't love' (pp.182–3). Mitchell's difficulty in believing Jack's protestations of love may well stem from old difficulties with his mother: 'Does she love me? How can I ever be sure? Is she a madonna or just a whore? Does she really love me, or is she just dealing with me as she might deal with any other physical object? Am I ever more than just another body in her life? To what extent must I 'do' in order to 'be'? Can I trust that Jack and I love each other without us constantly having sex to prove it?'

If no one helps us to think about ourselves as subjective beings, capable of intellectual thought and interesting feeling, our sense of ourselves remains rooted in our physical bodies. In these circumstances, writes Spinelli (2001), the danger is that 'The act has become a person [and] what we do, or do not do, has become who we are, or are not' (pp.90–1). If our formative 'sexual' experiences are with mothers, it may well be that Mitchell's original relationship with his mother remained a purely physical one. This might have been the only kind of relationship she could provide: changing his nappy, feeding him, changing him, feeding him. She may never have had time to sit with him, admiring and cherishing him, delighting in his baby smiles and gurgles, interested in his baby thoughts and feelings. The kind of love that Mitchell now seeks from Jack is insistently physical, perhaps because Mitchell doesn't trust that any other kind of love is possible or even exists.

Just as Winnicott (1965) writes about the inevitability of 'impingements', those unforeseen happenings that test a secure mother–child relationship, so Kernberg (1995) writes about 'discontinuities', the ways in which couples share a sexual experience and then separate. They can merge and then part happily, no longer needing to have sex until the next time. These 'discontinuities' don't destroy a mature relationship, argues Kernberg. Rather, they're inevitable and necessary. He links the idea of discontinuity back to a child experiencing its mother's interest returning to the father from the child, leaving the child confident that this separation isn't the end of everything but is perfectly tolerable because she'll return. My guess is that Mitchell's relationship with his mother didn't leave him with that inner confidence, which is why he remains desperate to merge with Jack and keep merging, unable to bear any discontinuity.

His relationship with me, on the other hand, is entirely built around discontinuity. We meet and we part. We meet a fortnight later. Then part again. I keep coming back: the mother who never loses interest. Like all young people, Mitchell is trying to live with frustration as an inevitable fact of life. He can't always get what he wants. 'People become real to us by frustrating us,' writes Phillips (2012), 'if they don't frustrate us they are merely figures of fantasy' (p.29). Nitsun (2006) agrees: 'How frustration and disappointment are dealt with is as much a part of sexuality as excitement and satisfaction' (p.36). In this respect, my working relationship with Mitchell will continue to be an important part of his learning. He and I don't have sex; we don't prove our relationship in that tangible way, and yet we're still pleased to see each other, we're still interested in each other, we still like each other. And we'll go on liking each other, no doubt, even when Mitchell frustrates me with his insistence that Jack is sexually abnormal and even when I frustrate Mitchell with my inability to make life simple.

5

LEARNING TO BE ALONE

HOW TO MERGE with someone and, at other times, be alone? How to be in a loving, sexual relationship and yet exist separately from the other person?

The theory is relatively straightforward. A baby with an attuned, attentive parent gradually internalizes the presence of that parent, no longer needing him or her to be physically present for the baby to know that it's never forgotten and, in that sense, never alone (Winnicott 1965). With enough of this experience, the baby is likely to grow up comfortable in his or her own company. But without enough of this experience, without ever being able to take the attention of other people for granted, the baby/child/young person will grow up feeling non-existent, terrified of being alone, clinging to other people, shouting for attention and, if necessary, seeking out confrontation as a desperate way of having some kind, *any* kind of relationship.

The fear of aloneness is a constant subtext in the behaviour of young people. It's a fear that affects the quality of their relationships, including their sexual relationships, because it can make being apart from other people – even temporarily – feel impossible. Whether the aloneness is social, psychological or sexual, young people's anxieties about it seep into everything: unconscious reminders of something they've experienced and don't want to experience again, an original baby-experience when they felt helpless, disconnected from the world, unable to attract anyone's attention, ignored by those around (Winnicott 1989). Young people dread the prospect of living through anything like that again, so when they meet with a counsellor, their first priority is to learn how to have happier, more loving, more fulfilling relationships. They're not interested in learning how to get better at being alone – far from it! And yet the quality of their relationships will always be informed by their ability to be alone.

Jake's dropped his sandwich in the school corridor where it lies messily.

I ask him to pick it up.

He looks at me fiercely. 'Why should I?'

'Because it's going to get trodden on at any moment.'

'So? I don't care. I don't want it!'

No doubt he worries that being seen by his friends to scoop up a soggy sandwich from the floor will be vaguely humiliating, but there's a part of him that simply won't take responsibility for this most mundane of incidents. His refusal to pick up the sandwich will get him into trouble but is, in part, a response to aloneness. It's his sandwich; he dropped it; he has to pick it up: no one's going to do it for him. It's his responsibility, but Jake's unwilling to take that responsibility. He'd rather get into trouble, which will give him a *social* experience involving arguments with me and possibly with other members of staff rather than pick up the sandwich which will be a brief but solitary experience.

It's a tiny incident in the school day and, of course, there's a lot more to know about Jake's relationship with authority-figures.

But young people feel alone in all sorts of daily situations and often struggle to deal with that experience, from getting up in the morning ('Do I have to?'), to going to school ('Do I have to?'), to getting on with homework ('Do I have to?'), to going to sleep ('Do I have to?'). These are mundane situations but situations where, however supportive the people around may be, no one can do it for young people: they're on their own, obliged to take responsibility for their own lives. Going to a party provokes far greater anxieties about aloneness: 'Will anyone recognize me? Will anyone talk to me? Will any of my friends be there?', while breaking up with a boyfriend or girlfriend provokes still greater anxieties: 'That's it! I'm going to be on my own for the rest of my life! No one's ever going to want to be with me again!'

Sensing how much this disturbs young people, parents sometimes use aloneness as a threat and punishment, isolating or sending sons and daughters to their rooms, taking away their phones. Schools and prisons have also always used aloneness as a threat and punishment. As a result, there are some young people who grow up to be compliant, desperate to please, doing anything to avoid aloneness for fear that it'll be imposed on them, while there are other young people, never left alone by their anxious parents and therefore never getting the chance to practise being alone. Still other young people grow up with aloneness as a modus vivendi: they become experts at avoiding eye contact, always staying on the sidelines, always keeping quiet. Because no one has ever taken any notice of them, they become so accustomed to being alone that the thought of company is terrifying. For them, any relationship involving trust and intimacy is a threat rather than a comfort or reassurance.

From the moment we're born, we start negotiating a pathway between merger and separation. Initially, that negotiation is with a mother or parent-figure: we want to be close to her, to be intimate and trusting, but, at the same time, we want to be independent, in need of no one, autonomous, solitary, proud. Gradually, we start learning where she ends and we begin and, in so doing, we start making sense of the world, making meaning. As Ogden (1986) writes, '... meaning requires difference, a dynamic relationship between an idea and that which it is not' (p.236). We learn that she has her own identity, that she's a person with a will of her own and not just a narcissistic extension of ourselves. We can influence her but not control her.

Caught up in all this, young people scorn the extremes of merger and separation: the shy boy still wholly dependent on his parents or the loner incapable of relationships; the couple whose friends complain that they're never apart ('It's like you're joined at the hip!') or the young person masturbating alone ('Wanker! You're such a wanker!'). No one congratulates the couple on their ability to commit to one another. No one congratulates the masturbator on his resourcefulness. And at home, most young people are giving their parents mixed messages: on the one hand 'I want you to help me!' but on the other hand 'I don't want you to help me!' All young people are practising, discovering how much separation, how much aloneness they can tolerate. Yalom (1980) writes from an existential perspective: 'The task of satisfying both needs – for separateness and autonomy and for protection and merger – and of facing the fear inherent in each, is a lifelong dialectic' (p.146). Glasser (1979) goes further, as I mentioned in the introduction to this book, identifying this as the 'core complex' at the heart of all our struggles.

So how do counsellors and other professionals help young people get better at being alone? At learning where one person ends and another begins? At learning how to be intimate and trusting while remaining independent and able to take personal responsibility? In sexual relationships, these dilemmas are endlessly enacted and re-enacted. Sex offers young people opportunities to practise selfishness and selflessness, to be simultaneously together and apart, each person able to initiate within the mutuality of the relationship. But sex can also be a refuge for young people desperate to escape the anxieties of being alone; young people with no real interest in each other, intent only on merging, merging, merging.

Seventeen-year-old Annie sits with me howling, gasping for breath, tears all over her face, not bothering to use the box of tissues beside her. '*Why?*' she wails, '*Why?*' Her normally articulate words have been replaced by childlike noises of bewilderment, fear and frustration. '*Why?*'

She's asking why her boyfriend has decided suddenly to finish with her.

I could say, 'Because people can be like that, Annie. They don't always understand. And sometimes they don't think. They don't realize how what they're doing is going to affect other people.' I could say all this but, right now, it would be pointless. She wouldn't hear. So I say nothing. I sit with her and wait. In effect, she's reminding herself of what she always knew: that there's nothing to be done, that this is how the world is, that we might have other people with us – in this case, a counsellor – which might feel fine but never takes away the brute fact that we're on our own, in relationships with lots of people while also being alone. At the moment, it's as if this normally articulate seventeen-year-old girl has become a seventeen-day-old or seventeen-month-old infant, unable to speak, terrified of the world and wanting to be held, scooped up in a parent's arms and comforted. Other seventeen-year-olds might regress to complete silence or might start hurling things around. Annie simply howls. I could scoop her up with comforting words but I judge that, for now, she can bear this panic with me alongside, implicitly supportive but in the background: part of her life but never able to change it.

Being with young people in counselling is like being a parent with a baby, constantly judging when to intervene and when to let the baby discover things for itself. New-born babies need a parent to intervene most of the time, taking charge, making all the practical decisions. But there are also times when the parent simply sits with the baby, reflecting back its sounds and facial expressions, extending them and adding new ones. There are times when the parent judges that the baby can be left for a minute to gaze at the ceiling while he or she goes to make a cup of coffee. Leave the baby for too long and it'll panic. Never leave the baby and it'll only ever recognize the face and voice of one person. The aim is to hold the baby securely in a relationship while also giving it opportunities to explore for itself. Parents never stop making judgments about when and how much is enough: how much relationship and how much aloneness a baby can tolerate. Hobson (1985) calls it 'aloneness-togetherness' where, in a therapeutic relationship, 'there is an apprehension of distinction and of mutuality, of autonomy and of reciprocity, of identity and of sharing' (p.26).

Young people bring to counselling an experience of 'aloneness-togetherness' in their lives so far. At the extremes, some will come expecting to get nothing whatsoever back from a counsellor, while others will expect the counsellor to do all the work. Annie brings to counselling a perfectly adequate experience of aloneness-togetherness which will have developed from the beginning of her life: she can listen and she can talk; she can initiate and she can allow me to initiate. It's just that, from time to time, when life gets tough, she panics, and when she panics, she regresses.

'*Why?*' she asks, glaring. '*Why* does he have to be like this? Surely he knew what it was going to be like for me? He's not stupid. So *why?*'

As a seventeen-year-old, she knows perfectly well that people can be cruel as well as kind. But as a seventeen-day-old baby or seventeen-month-old child, she can't answer her question. *Why?* Appealing to a seventeen-day-old baby's rational mind ('Well, it's because people can be cruel as well as kind, Annie…') would, indeed, be pointless.

However, she's starting to rediscover her words, as if she's growing up again, leaving behind her howling, panic-stricken baby-state. 'I suppose there's no answer,' she volunteers. 'He's just a bastard!'

'It's tough,' I say. 'Tough when people behave badly.'

The context is important. In a few weeks' time, Annie will be taking exams and, after that time, our sessions will finish because she'll be leaving school. For her, the prospect of aloneness is everywhere, from going into the exam hall on her own, her academic life in her hands, to leaving school in a few weeks and (as she says) the 'whole weirdness' of that. For most young people, leaving school throws up old anxieties about leaving mother-figures (Luxmoore 2008). In the weeks and months before leaving, they regress intermittently: they feel like giving up; they fall out with their friends; they panic. So it's not surprising that Annie is revisiting anxieties about aloneness at this time in her life, as if she's a baby, wondering all over again, 'Does anyone notice me, hear me? Does anyone understand me, think about me? Am I worth anything to anyone?'

She wipes her face. 'I know there's nothing I can do. I know I have to deal with it ...'

I ask, 'What's it like when you're alone, Annie?'

'Fine, most of the time,' she says, 'except when he doesn't reply to my texts. Or when my friends have all gone out and haven't invited me. That's not fine!'

'What does it feel like?'

'Like no one wants to be with me. Like I'm worthless. Like I don't exist ...' Again she looks panic-stricken. 'Can we not talk about this?'

I explain that I'm asking because being alone *can* feel horrible and we tend to think that we're the only people feeling it. 'But it's important to be alone sometimes,' I say. 'Not because it's good to have horrible experiences, but because in lots of ways we *are* alone and have to get used to it. In our relationship here, in this room, we're together but also alone. Sometimes we might feel very together and very connected and at other times we might feel very alone and disconnected. That's normal. It's like being connected to another person *and* alone.'

Winnicott (1971) would describe our conversation as a kind of playing together. Like a parent and child, we take turns, sometimes anticipating each other, sometimes frustrating each other. It's what he calls the 'potential' or 'intermediate' space wherein counsellor and client try things out, practising being together and apart, understanding each other and not understanding each other. If a young person begins a counselling relationship in a baby-state, the counsellor will, like a parent, need to take control, initiating all the conversations and steering them in certain directions in anticipation of the young person's need. But as the young person grows up within the relationship, the power will increasingly need to be negotiated and shared as the young person learns to bear the ups and downs of the relationship with all its satisfactions and limitations. In this sense, the young person is learning what it feels like to be alone sometimes (frustrated, relaxed, angry, calm, lost, happy) while still connected. At the end of each session, he or she goes away, physically alone but remembered, as if the counsellor is implicitly saying, 'I'll still be thinking of you. See you next week!'

Sometimes young people regress and then grow up again within the space of a single counselling session. In response to my comment about being connected *and* alone, Annie says that she understands. 'I worry that I'm not normal, though. I mean, you don't see other people crying all the time like this, do you!'

I suggest to her that they might cry in private.

'I doubt it!' she says. 'Don't tell me they spend all their time having meltdowns like I do! They're just better at dealing with stuff.'

She's tussling, beginning to challenge me now as an independent seventeen-year-old. In Winnicott's terms, we're playing together as adults: Annie's no longer my baby and I'm no longer her parent.

I say that I admire her ability to be honest about how scared she feels.

'You mean, like when I come here and lose the plot?'

'No, I mean when you're being honest about how you feel and about how upsetting things are.'

'That's because they *are* upsetting,' she says. 'Especially when stuff happens and there's nothing you can do.'

Her grandmother died of cancer nine months ago. I ask if that's what she's referring to.

'Not just that,' she says, 'but everything. All the crap...'

For babies, the world is a mother who does or doesn't make things safe. But for a sophisticated seventeen-year-old, the world has become a whole set of variables: some good, some bad; some within a person's control, some not; some understandable and some that make no sense whatsoever, like people dying. Annie's also aware of an existential aloneness.

She goes on, 'All the crap in the world that doesn't make sense. All the pointless crap!'

I say nothing.

She's quiet, thinking.

At the start of counselling relationships, silence can be disturbing. For those young people with little or no internalized sense of being connected to other people, the threat of non-existence is ever-present and the need for another person's verbal presence is desperate. An ability to tolerate silence in counselling is an ability to tolerate aloneness: when they feel connected, young people can bear silence; when they don't feel connected, they can't. My silence with Annie feels comfortable at the moment but that may quickly change. Sometimes I break the silence myself as evidence that our relationship is fluid, mutual, not bound by rigid rules: we share responsibility for initiating conversation.

I remind her that we have three more meetings before she leaves school.

Still she says nothing, still thinking, then starts telling me about an old film she's seen. A teenage girl and her much younger brother are lost in the Australian desert after their father tries to kill them. They get more and more lost until they meet an Aboriginal boy who's on 'walkabout', forced to survive by himself as part of his initiation into adulthood. He teaches them to survive before eventually leading them back to the city.

I ask what made her think of this film.

'It's quite scary at first,' she says, 'because they're lost and you think they're going to die. And the girl's trying her best but she hasn't got a clue. And then at the end of the film she's grown up and living in the city with a really boring husband, and you can see her thinking about the past and about what happened when they were alone in the desert and how she misses it. How it was just her and her brother and the Aborigine boy, and they didn't really need anyone else. They were okay on their own.'

I ask her if she feels like the girl in the film.

She laughs at me. 'God,' she says, 'you're such a *counsellor* sometimes!'

6

SHAME AND PRIVACY

IF THE FEAR of being alone haunts young people, then the fear of being cast out and publicly humiliated is even worse.

Kerry hasn't been to school since it happened. In fact, according to her mother, Kerry's been refusing to go anywhere near school: staying at home all day, crying in her room, refusing to eat or even get dressed. And the worst thing is that everybody – *everybody* – knows why.

She's come to see me as a prelude to starting back at school. 'I know I've got to go back,' she says. 'Everyone's been on at me all the time – my family and that attendance woman. They all say it wasn't my fault. But I know what it'll be like when I go back. Everyone's going to be saying stuff and laughing and having a go at me…' She starts crying. 'My life's ruined!'

I let her cry. 'It was a horrible thing that happened, Kerry. And horrible the way everyone always reacts, as if what happened was somehow okay and as if they've never made a mistake or done anything they regret.'

'I know it was stupid!' she says. 'I know that! And I'll never do anything like it again. But they'll never forget. I know they won't! Everyone at school knows. Even the teachers! Everyone's going to be looking at me and knowing what happened!'

She and her friend were hanging out with a group of older boys in the park, drinking vodka and (although she hasn't said this) probably enjoying the attentions of the older boys. Apparently Kerry and one of the boys went a short distance away from the others and she ended up giving him a blow-job, something she'd never done before (Kerry is a virgin), didn't want to do and hated doing. When they rejoined the group, the boy immediately told his friends and, within hours, the whole world knew.

'Nobody says anything about him!' she continues, still crying. 'Nobody has a go at him or calls him names. Oh, no! His mates just think it's funny. He can go round saying what he likes and everyone believes him!'

She's wrong and she's right. When Kerry finally admitted what had happened, her mother phoned the police who have since interviewed the boy and are now in the process of deciding what to do. In the UK, consensual sex is defined as 'active and passionate' which this clearly wasn't. Non-consensual oral penetration is classified as rape in exactly the same way as vaginal or anal penetration. The police will do something. So she's wrong in saying that no one disapproves of what the boy did and that everyone believes his side of the story. At school, members of staff are also making clear their outrage about what the boy did to Kerry.

However, she's right in guessing that many of her peers will have a less sympathetic attitude. There's still an assumption that, if bad things happen, it's because girls are somehow 'asking for it' whereas boys are only being boys (Coy *et al.* 2013). Unfortunately, many of her peers will be enjoying the story with a vested interest in it: boys hiding own their private fear of humiliation by publicly humiliating girls; girls vilifying Kerry without acknowledging their own prurient interest in other people's sexual business... So many young people exploring dilemmas of their own about trust, intimacy, consent, shame and privacy through poor Kerry, the latest young person to be set up and attacked for getting it wrong. In situations like this, young people habitually attack because they're habitually afraid. 'To what extent am I ever in control of my own life?' they might be asking. 'What part should sex play in my life? How much of what happens to me should I share with other people and how much should I keep to myself? And if, one day, something happens to me like what happened to Kerry, what would I do?'

'I feel disgusting,' says Kerry, still tearful, 'like I'm dirty or something. I know that might sound stupid but it's how I've been feeling since it happened.'

It'll take a long time for her to regain her confidence. Gilligan (2000) notes that 'Since one's sexual identity is such a central constituent of a person's sense of self, if it is destroyed, so is the self' (p.152). It would be easy to give Kerry advice, telling her to be wary of going with boys to the park and suggesting strategies for dealing with similar situations in the future. She'll have already learned bitter lessons and, in any case, straightforward behavioural suggestions like these imply that we have no unconscious, private life: only an external, objective life about which we only ever make conscious choices. One of the reasons why we're so suspicious of other people's privacy, argues Cohen (2013), is that we like to pretend that we can make straightforward choices in a straightforward world. 'You like your sexuality where you can see it,' he jokes. 'If you can't, you prefer to say it's not there' (p.100). What I imagine will be especially hard for Kerry to talk about is that part of her will have been curious about the boys in the park, wondering what they'd be like sexually and whether they'd find her attractive. This doesn't excuse the boy for doing what he did. Nor does it excuse the other boys for mocking Kerry and suggesting that somehow what happened was her fault. It wasn't. And for anyone to suggest that, in some way, she deserved what happened would be disgraceful. But like other young people, Kerry will have *wondered* about sex as her own body started changing; she'll have tried on make-up, curious about its effects on people; she'll have tried on clothes to see how glamorous they made her look. Like any young person, she'll have been interested to know more about herself as a sexual person... These things will have been hard to admit before any of this happened and even harder to admit now.

Fortunately, she has two friends who have stood by her and, fortunately, her mother hasn't made things worse by adding to Kerry's sense of shame. So the chances are that she'll make it back to school and we'll continue meeting. But going back to school, I agree with her, will definitely be scary and, for a while, she'll feel nervous wherever she happens to be, half-expecting to hear muttered comments in the corridor ('Slag! Whore! Dog! Slut!') or loud swallowing noises and requests for blow-jobs shouted out from the safety of the crowd. Shame hurts. Especially when it's undeserved.

Kerry's only thirteen. Like so many young people, she's learning hard lessons about who to trust and how to manage her privacy. She's also learning about the way boys sometimes behave because, in hers as in so many stories, it's the girl who's shamed, the girl who gets called names, the girl who's made to feel dirty. Never the boy. Yet whenever a boy has his trousers pulled down in public or must endure endless jokes about the size of his penis, it's as humiliating for him as many of the experiences girls endure. Boys traditionally (and sometimes collectively) turn their humiliation into hostility, taking it out on other boys who seem vulnerable or taking it out on girls like Kerry. I would imagine that the sixteen-year-old boy who took Kerry to one side, pretending to like her before getting her to give him a blow-job and then telling his friends, probably had an acute sense of his own vulnerability buried beneath a swaggering, macho, couldn't-care-less façade. Diamond (2014) describes just such a person who 'disowns his feelings of being utterly helpless and vulnerable by making the other person feel these emotions. The eroticized pleasure is associated with the achievement of "total" control, of being in the position of master of what is happening' (p.287).

We'd condemn what the boy did with Kerry as we'd condemn the behaviour of his friends, laughing and sneering and asking her what she's charging in order to deflect from their own secret sense of humiliation. When a boy refers to a girl as 'it' rather than 'she', we tell him how disrespectful he's being. When boys refer to girls, not in terms of their personalities, but in terms of their bodies, especially their sexual bodies, we say how wrong that is. How wrong, how disrespectful, how rude. The boys walk off, bristling. But Horne (2012) is right: 'Difficult as it might be, with many boys we need to be able to view verbal abuse, often with very disparaging sexual language, as a way of expressing anxiety and often fear' (p.95). Chodorow (1989) suggests that, because a boy is usually brought up by a mother, he fears the abiding power of her femininity and so, in order to identify himself as a man, in order to be separate from her, he distances himself and from anything remotely 'feminine' with displays of vehement disgust and hostility: 'Slag! Whore! Dog! Slut!'

In my experience, many boys don't just objectify girls and women: they objectify everything. And they do it because they can't bear their own subjective experience. It's as if the possibility of having an internal life of their own, full of fears and doubts and private thoughts, is too much to bear. So all that internal, scary stuff gets projected out, re-presented as something tangible, as a thing to be dismissed rather than as a feeling to be experienced. This happens most obviously in bullying where one person's anxiety about being small or weak is attributed to another person and attacked. *He's* small and weak – not me! *She's* dirty – not me!

I remember one boy who'd experienced more than his fair share of hurt and shame: attachments ripped apart, promises made and repeatedly broken. Unable to bear the feelings he was left with, Lenny acted them out at other people's expense and, as a result, was forever in trouble with school and with the police. He couldn't talk about any of this. Whenever I asked about anything personal, whenever I asked about how he was feeling, he couldn't say. He'd look away, ashamed and angry, frustrated, not knowing where to begin. However, when we talked about his favourite football team, he came alive. He knew everything about the players. He knew about their opponents, tactics, scores and scorers. He could describe the team's ups and downs, hopes and fears, strengths and weaknesses. The team became an objectification of everything that Lenny himself would have been feeling and thinking if ever he could have allowed himself to feel and to think. He could talk about football, but when I asked how things had been at home, he couldn't speak.

'How's your mum?'

'Okay.'

'Is she still with Garry?'

'Yeah...'

'What's that like for you?'

'Okay.'

Boys (and men) objectify girls (and women) because they can't bear to feel their own fear, their own longing for intimacy, their own vulnerability and need for tenderness. They can control something physical but can't control a feeling or a fear (Jukes 1993). So of course we disapprove of the offensive language, the sexualization of relationships and the treatment of girls like Kerry as commodities, but it's important to remember that boys do it because it's often the only thing they know to do when no one has ever supported them in experiencing themselves subjectively. Rather than ask small boys what they're feeling, we ask them what they're doing; rather than ask them about their fears and sadnesses and longings, we praise their bravery, their energy, their physicality. They end up objectifying relationships because they've been objectified themselves from an early age. They grow into young men intent on making sex mechanical in order *not* to empathize with the other person because to empathize is to surrender some degree of control by taking another person's feelings and needs into account. And control is everything for boys threatened with humiliation: the humiliation of having your genitals visible outside rather than hidden inside your body, of being expected to be big and strong when you feel small and weak, of having to act as if you're experienced when you know that you're inexperienced, of having to masturbate regularly simply to deal with so much testosterone. Fighting other boys is one way of externalizing these internal fights. The boy who humiliated Kerry was probably jealous of her innocence and probably enjoyed spoiling things for her. He probably enjoyed his feeling of being in control and was relieved that the humiliation ended up being hers rather than his.

He'll also have hated himself. I met with Lenny for two years: two years of football talk mixed with speculation about what each of the players and the team manager (the parent-figure) might be feeling; two years of sharing bits of my own emotional experience in order to model for Lenny that it might be possible to be a football fan and yet feel vulnerable sometimes; two years of helping him bear the thought that he might be strong *and* weak, brave *and* afraid, powerful *and* powerless. Whenever I asked him about love ('Have you got people who want to go out with you, Lenny?') he'd bat away my enquiry, saying that he hadn't got time for any of that stuff. Whenever I asked him about how things were with his mum, he'd go quiet.

'It's hard, Lenny, when people make mistakes and there's nothing we can do to help them…'

'I wouldn't know, really. It's my mum's life! It's up to her!'

'I know. But hard for you, I guess, when you care about her and can't do anything to protect her.'

'Like I said, it's her life. She can do what she wants!'

'And she'll probably never know how much you care about her or how hurtful it feels for you, seeing her when she's upset…'

He didn't reply, but his agreement was tacit. And this much was news, Lenny admitting to feeling hurt sometimes! This much was progress!

'It's tempting to take it out on other people, Lenny. Tempting to take all our hurt and hatred and go and beat the crap out of someone…'

He nodded and seemed to be thinking about this. More progress.

'And people will never know what you really feel because you're such an expert at hiding stuff…'

'Did you watch the match at the weekend?'

Perhaps of more importance than Lenny's occasional readiness to acknowledge what he might be feeling was the fact that we kept meeting, with all that our meeting implied: that we liked each other, that he was interested in talking to someone and that he needed to talk in the first place. For many young people, acknowledging their need for others is fraught with anxiety, caught as they are between a desire for independence ('You can't tell me what to do!') and a desire for dependence ('Just tell me what to do!'), between separating from their parents and remaining merged with them. It's a messy business, lurching backwards and forwards between one need and another when independence and dependence are *both* necessary. It's much easier for young people to split themselves into one thing or the other. It simplifies and appears to make things clearer: 'Either I need my parents or I don't need my parents… Either I love you or I hate you… Either I'm straight or I'm gay…' As a counsellor, I'm always encouraged when young people declare themselves to be bisexual. Good, I think. You're resisting the temptation to simplify yourself and managing to bear the anxiety of things not always being completely clear.

'Either I'm a public or a private person…' is another simplification. 'Either everything's out in the open or everything's secret…' Cohen (2013) describes the popular assumption that anything kept private must be bad and must be made public as soon as possible. As I've written elsewhere (Luxmoore 2000), young people have to learn that there are *degrees* of privacy, that they might tell some people some things and other people other things, that keeping some things to oneself isn't dishonest or the sign of being a bad friend. It's normal.

But learning this takes practice. Lenny kept everything to himself, risking nothing, impassive. Other young people keep nothing to themselves, telling everyone everything and then wishing they hadn't as the misunderstandings and arguments erupt.

Kerry is learning her own hard lessons about privacy and, in particular, about sexual privacy.

'Whenever I see the boys,' she says, 'I'm going to know exactly what they're thinking. They think they're so clever. But how would they like it if someone did that to one of their sisters?'

'Presumably you thought you could trust the boy?'

'Yeah, because I didn't know that was what he wanted. I just thought we were going for a chat.'

'Like a boyfriend and girlfriend?'

'No, not like that,' she says. 'It wasn't like we were going out or anything. But I did think he liked me. He was telling me stuff about being a carer for his mum because he hasn't got a dad, and looking after her all the time, and I could see he was getting upset. I was feeling really sorry for him. I thought he wanted to talk...'

We pause. I decide not to ask about what exactly happened in the park. Our relationship is too recent and Kerry needs to be allowed to cover up, having been rushed into something she didn't want to do. In counselling she needs to remain in control and *not* feel obliged to do or say anything to anyone. She needs an experience of her privacy being respected and of privacy itself being a *necessary* thing, never an obstacle, never a problem. Some young people are understandably afraid of counselling because it threatens to strip away their privacy and leave them exposed, while others sit with a counsellor and tell everything without regard for confidentiality or trust, promiscuous in their storytelling.

Counselling is an opportunity for young people to practise privacy: going slowly, telling some things and not others. In effect, counsellors are privacy coaches, respecting a young person's defences as he or she – always afraid of being shamed – tests the relationship, takes a few calculated risks while retaining plenty of control. One of a child's earliest games is peek-a-boo: hiding behind a hand or toy or piece of furniture and re-appearing with a cry of 'Boo!' Developmentally, the game is important, suggesting to the child that he or she can be unseen yet not forgotten and that the other person playing the game can disappear yet not be gone. Winnicott (1965) describes 'a child establishing a private self that is not communicating, and at the same time wanting to communicate and to be found. It is a sophisticated game of hide-and-seek in which it is a joy to be hidden but disaster not to be found' (p.186). This characterizes the behaviour of so many young people. For Kerry, for Lenny and for other young people coming anxiously to counselling, it's a joy to be able to hide from the counsellor but, equally, a disaster not to be found. Flirting with boys in a park, Kerry was essentially playing her own game of hide-and-seek. She might not have wanted to stay hidden for the rest of her life but, at that moment, certainly didn't want to be found.

For many young people, sex becomes a focus for anxieties about privacy. In the beginning, two eleven-year-olds stand next to each other in the playground. They barely know each other's names but, officially, they're 'going out'. Life is simple.

A year later, two twelve-year-olds are holding hands shyly and daring to kiss for the first time, surrounded by noisy friends and a frenzy of sexual suggestion. Life is becoming more complicated...

Melanie's fifteen. I make her a cup of hot chocolate about which she's quite specific: three teaspoons of chocolate, some milk and two sugars. I stir the drink thoroughly, put it on the table next to her, sit down and ask how things have been since we last met. Twenty minutes later, I notice that she hasn't touched her drink. Because this often happens when young people are caught up in telling their stories, I remind her, 'Don't forget your drink!'

She looks doubtful. 'I don't want it.'

'Not thirsty?'

'It's not that,' she says, embarrassed. 'I just don't like it when people are watching me drink.'

I'm reminded of other young people who say they hate being seen. 'What if I look away, Melanie?'

'No, that won't make any difference. Sorry.'

I wonder what's going on. Lots of boys want to go out with Melanie but, whenever I've asked about this, she's been scornful, aware that their intentions will probably be dishonourable. Yet one of the reasons why she's here, one of the concerns for members of staff who suggested that she meet with me, is that she's been sending naked pictures of herself to boys, allowing herself to be well and truly seen. Inevitably, these pictures have been forwarded to dozens of other people. So on the one hand, Melanie doesn't even like to be seen drinking hot chocolate and, guarding her privacy, can see straight through the lustful banter of boys, but on the other hand, she's been sending naked pictures of herself to people as if her privacy was of no consequence at all.

Of the many ideas about what constitutes a sense of 'self' (Luxmoore 2008), Kohut's (1977) idea is that a 'self' is best thought about as a collection of internalized relationships he calls 'selfobjects'. Our relationship with a mother becomes part of who we are; our relationship with a father or sibling or friend adds to the sum of who we are. We become the important relationships we've absorbed over the years. Kohut argues that inappropriate, sexualized behaviour is therefore a way of dealing with some disturbance of the 'core self', a way of dealing with the lack of good, internalized relationships to which a person can attach and feel safe. 'In order to escape from depression,' he writes, 'the child turns from the unempathic or absent selfobject to oral, anal and phallic sensations' (p.122). Melanie isn't a child and has long since moved on from any oral, anal or phallic preoccupations she may have had when she was small. Nevertheless, sending boys naked pictures of herself might have been her defence against a whole range of difficult feelings: feelings of emptiness, sadness and hatred as well as feelings of love and longing (Alvarez 2012). Taking naked pictures of herself might have been an attempt to bolster up a fragmented sense of herself, as if she was trying to hold herself together by making a tangible picture of herself, a photograph, and by concentrating on the sexual titillation of that. 'Takes your mind off things!' she might have said at the time, relieved perhaps no longer to be feeling so empty, so alone or unloved.

Diamond (2014) agrees with Kohut, arguing that 'eroticisation can be defensive, a means of trying to deal with emotional disturbances originating in early failures and difficulties in the attachment relationship' (p.285). Melanie certainly has reason to feel empty, alone and unloved. Her father left to live with another woman, then came home, then left again. Nowadays she sees him only occasionally. He continues to promise great things and always breaks his promises. She could refuse to see him altogether, but then she'd have no father. So she guards herself against further hurt by taking a sceptical view of her father and of lustful boys making promises, yet still she sends those boys naked pictures of herself. It's as if she wants all the flirtation and excitement of sex, yet wants none of it. Sex takes her mind off things. Paradoxically, sex might help her to feel stronger so that she no longer needs sex.

She offers me a knowing half-smile, playful but keeping her distance.

'I know you don't let these things get to you,' I say to her, 'but it must have hurt when you were younger and your father kept breaking his promises?'

'Not really,' she says, tight-lipped. 'You get used to it.'

'Get used to feeling hurt? To feeling angry? To feeling ashamed of him?'

'I admit I used to get pissed off,' she says. 'I used to cry sometimes when I was little and I'd be waiting for him and he wouldn't turn up. But that's just my dad. I've got better things to do with my life!'

She keeps returning our conversation to the present. My guess is that she's much more damaged than her usually confident, cheeky exterior would suggest. Her father had a string of affairs after finally leaving Melanie and her mother. Two of these affairs produced Melanie's half-siblings. Interestingly, Mollon (2001), in writing about Kohut's ideas, suggests that the children of parents whose relationship has been destroyed by sexual desire may well come to think of their own sexual desirability as the thing that will most attract and endear them to other people in the future.

Melanie tells me a story about one of her friends whose boyfriend has been cheating. 'I told her she's stupid to take him back after what he'd gone and done to her. I told her there's nothing wrong with being single. You can flirt with boys. Doesn't mean you've got to go with them!'

Again, that knowing half-smile, as if she's flirting with me, flirting with the idea of trusting me, attaching to me. Perhaps flirting is the only way she knows of relating to someone – never quite sure how much to trust the other person, offering something but always holding something back. Echoing Kohut, Lemma *et al.* (2011) propose that the 'Sexualisation of the therapeutic relationship is often used as a means of resisting feelings of vulnerability and powerlessness' (p.194). Potentially, our conversation gives Melanie a chance to say what she *isn't* normally able to say but might nevertheless be feeling (vulnerable? powerless?) in the expectation that the tension might lessen between her sexualized defence (her flirting) and the damage to Melanie that it protects.

The next time we meet, I check that she'll drink her hot chocolate if I make it.

She says she will. 'Sometimes I just get weird,' she says, 'like last time. I'm not like it all the time.'

We talk, stories from the last week mixed with stories from when she was younger. In Winnicott's (1965) terms, we're accepting her 'false self' as necessary and permissible – nothing to be ashamed about – while allowing her 'real self' gradually to emerge and be seen. Counselling is never about breaking down a person's defences in order to reveal some quintessential truth. Therapy isn't confession. Yet there are young people who feel ashamed of their own privacy, worrying that they should be telling everything to everyone

– especially to a counsellor – because that's what normal people do. It isn't.

Melanie used her phone to send the pictures. Lee (2013) recommends that counsellors encourage young people to bring their phones into counselling because, in effect, young people will be bringing in a part of themselves that needs decoding and thinking about: a part of themselves clogged up with advice, insults, gossip and endless conversation. I suggest to Melanie that I'd be very happy to see some of the written messages on her phone but *only* if she wants to show me and only if she thinks it might be helpful to look at them together. 'You don't have to show me anything, Melanie.'

'I know,' she says. 'I do know that!'

Writing about shame, Mollon (2002) describes the shame surrounding a false self (the pretence of not caring, for example, or the pretence of being sexually confident), a shame born of the belief that a more 'real' self would never be recognized, would never be understood or accepted by other people. 'Shame arises both from violation of the self', he writes, '*and* from exposure of the self when this is not met with the expected or hoped for empathy' (p.20). So Melanie might well be ashamed of sending naked pictures of herself to boys, but might feel that she had no choice because no one would otherwise take any notice of her as a shy or sexually unconfident person. 'I exist only when I'm seen,' she might be saying to the world, 'and when I can't be seen, it's as if I don't exist.'

I know that she's been looking forward to her grandmother's seventieth birthday party, at which various members of her family will be together in the same room for the first time in ages.

'But I might not be going now,' she says, 'because me and Mum had an argument. I asked if my boyfriend could come and she said no, so I went off on one!'

'Swearing?'

'Yeah!'

'Swearing like, "If he's not coming, Mum, then I'm not going to any fucking party and there's nothing you can do to make me?"'

She smiles, acknowledging that, yes, this is more or less exactly what she said to her mother.

'In fact, Mum,' I continue, 'you can stick the fucking party right up your fucking arse!'

She laughs out loud. We both laugh and it's as if our laughter defuses something. It's as if, hearing her words mirrored back to her, Melanie is able to laugh at herself, at how silly it all sounds; how silly and pointless and true. It's as if she's stepping back and looking at herself: her grown-up, fifteen-year-old-self looking and laughing at her child-self having a tantrum. In effect, she's *reflecting on herself*: the therapeutic grail for counsellors working with young people whose difficulty is that they've never learned to reflect on themselves because, from the day they were born, no one took the time to sit with them, carefully imitating their expressions and sounds, reflecting them back to themselves until they learned to reflect on themselves (Luxmoore 2008).

I ask Melanie about her boyfriend. How can she tell whether or not he's interested in her as a person rather than as someone simply to use for sex. We talk about her needing to develop a really good Bullshit Detector and I suggest to her that she should keep her Bullshit Detector with her at all times, day and night. She laughs. We joke about the cheesy chat-up lines boys use.

I ask, 'Did it hurt?'

She looks puzzled. 'When?'

'When you fell from heaven?'

She gets the joke. Together we chorus, 'BULLSHIT DETECTOR!'

When Kerry, still recovering from what happened with the boy in the park, develops an efficient Bullshit Detector of her own, she'll feel safer and more confident, able to see through boys who tell a tragic tale ('Poor me, looking after my poor disabled mum!') at the same time as they want to get girls into bed. Privacy is one of the ways in which we protect ourselves from shame, and shame is what young people fear more than anything else. Shame makes young people want to kill themselves.

Naz has been thinking about killing himself, he says, ever since splitting up with Katie. She was everything. His life revolved around her and, now that she's gone, it feels as if he's got nothing left. While he was with her, he scarcely bothered with ordinary friendships, his mother having long since left and his relationship with his father having only ever been perfunctory. Now he tortures himself with recriminations, with all the things he might have said and done differently. He imagines who Katie might be with right now and whether she might have started loving someone else.

Of course there'll be ways in which the loss of Katie echoes and replays the loss of his mother and we'll talk about that. There'll probably be ways in which Katie became idealized as a counter-balance to Naz's demonizing of his mother (Jukes 1993), but sometimes 'I feel suicidal' means 'I feel ashamed'. The defence that Naz constructed for himself (his relationship with Katie) has been torn away and he's been left exposed – alone, empty, unloved. Feeling suicidal makes sense as a way of wanting to make the shame go away.

Together we'll bear the shame. In counselling, at least, he'll be an interesting, likeable person. We'll talk about Katie and about his mother, but we'll also talk about friends, about what happens from week to week in Naz's life and about his occasional enthusiasms – poker, rap music and internet games. We won't ignore the losses in his life but these everyday things will be just as interesting because, torn apart, Naz has to put himself back together in a more flexible, less all-or-nothing way.

'Everyone knows!' he says. 'Everyone looks at me! I haven't got anyone to talk to any more! I've got nothing! I might as well be dead!'

He sounds like Kerry in the aftermath of her experience in the park. It's as if Naz has gone from feeling wonderfully private, cocooned in his relationship with Katie, to feeling horribly public.

'Maybe your old self has died, Naz? Your old self who loved and depended on Katie? Who didn't need anyone else? Maybe now you're becoming a new person – still loving, still kind, but probably more careful than before. And my guess is that when people get to meet this person, they'll like him. But you don't know that yet…'

Mollon (2002) argues that, deep down, shame comes from the feeling of not being able to connect with other people and, originally, from not being able to connect with a mother. The baby who feels unnoticed and unrecognized will panic, feeling as if it doesn't exist, as if it's worthless, as if it might as well be dead. I promise Naz that we'll meet again next week; that we'll stay connected.

Buckland brings to counselling a different experience of not being able to connect. He can't ejaculate inside his girlfriend. Everything else is fine, he says. His girlfriend enjoys the sex, but is perturbed. And so is he.

I'm touched by his courage in talking about this. We discuss what happens physically and everything sounds straightforward. He can ejaculate perfectly well after withdrawing from his girlfriend. We discuss family dynamics, wondering together about what else might be going on for him: his relationship with his parents, the critical voices in his head, his memories and doubts, his sense of the future. But again, everything sounds relatively straightforward.

Then one week he comes in and it's happened. He did it.

I ask what, if anything, made the difference.

'I think it was you saying about 'mess', he says. 'Something about that word. It just made sense.'

I cast my mind back. We'd been talking about the messiness of sex, about what it would be like to know that his semen was inside his girlfriend, whether it would feel like he'd made a mess or messed her up in some way. I remembered saying rather tritely that so many things in life end up being a mess.

I'm sure there were other things contributing to the change in Buckland's fortunes. But one way of understanding privacy is that it describes something of our ability to separate from or remain connected with other people. 'How much of myself do I share and how much do I keep back?' And 'mess' might describe our uncertainty about this, our ambivalence about control and surrender. Buckland's mess may have been particular to him, but other young people like Kerry, like Lenny, like Melanie and like Naz find themselves in other kinds of messes, all of which are about the boundary between doing it and not doing it, saying it and not saying it: the boundary between complete openness and complete secrecy. Learning to manage privacy is a messy business.

7

MOTHERS AND FATHERS

PARENTS INFLUENCE US powerfully and subtly. Some parents are keen to talk with their children about sex while others avoid the subject altogether. Some issue stern moral injunctions while others are blithely permissive. Most young people eventually embark on their sexual journey with a sense of what their parents happen to think about sex and sexual behaviour. But a much greater influence on those young people is their experience of their parents as sexual beings.

From birth, we see them with and without each other, touching or not touching, talking fondly or disparagingly about each other. We store these observations alongside our own relationships with them: tactile or not, affectionate or not, trusting or not, intimate or not… Unconsciously, these experiences are assimilated by any young person growing up and are far more influential than any advice; they affect a young person's sexual confidence and identity far more decisively.

I ask Ahmet, 'What are they like together, your mum and dad?'

'I don't know,' he says. 'What do you mean?'

'I mean do they hug? Do they kiss? Do they laugh?'

'I don't know,' he says, squirming. 'They do sometimes, I suppose, but I wouldn't really know. I'm not around much!'

I think what he means is that this is really hard to talk about. And really embarrassing. And can we please get back to talking about his girlfriend and how they nearly split up and how he doesn't know whether he can ever trust her again?

'Our parents are important,' I explain. 'They give us our confidence or they take it away. And usually we carry them around in our heads and they affect how we are with other people.'

He doesn't understand.

'For example, the way you are with Nelly might be a bit like the way your dad is with your mum ... ?'

'But I'm nothing like my dad!' says Ahmet indignantly. 'And I wouldn't want to be like him. No way! I'm completely different. He just sits there looking at his phone every evening, eating whatever Mum's made and drinking beer. That's all he does! And then he gets all paranoid and tries to stop her going out of the house in case she meets someone!'

'Like he doesn't trust her...'

'Exactly!'

I decide not to make any connection at this stage between Ahmet who doesn't trust his girlfriend and Ahmet's father who doesn't trust Ahmet's mother. We need to develop a more nuanced understanding of his father before thinking about whether Ahmet might be like him in any way. His father will have reasons for fearing that Ahmet's mother might leave: reasons that possibly go back to earlier losses in his own life or to cultural assumptions about men controlling women. Only once we understand our parents compassionately can we bear to acknowledge the ways in which we might – just possibly – be like them, and like them in ways we never planned or imagined possible.

Laura has all sorts of other things she wants to talk about – her friends, pets, teachers, siblings, enemies…plus a father who lives on his own, drinks and is depressed. Laura worries about how she looks, about being betrayed by her friends, and about whether or not to go out with certain boys.

She's thirteen. She lives with her mother who's thirty-two, a younger sister and two much younger half-brothers, each of whom have different fathers. Also living with them is her mother's new boyfriend, Simon, who's twenty-four.

'Simon's okay,' she says. 'He hasn't got a job or anything, but he makes Mum laugh and keeps her happy. I don't mind him really.'

Laura's come to see me because she's been cutting her arms and getting into trouble at school. She says she doesn't know why she cuts but does know why she gets into trouble.

'It's the teachers!' she says. 'They're pathetic! They're always picking on me for stuff I haven't done. I hate them!'

I suggest to her that, apart from teachers, she's got plenty of other things in her life to be angry about.

She's not interested in this. She wants to talk about teachers.

I suggest that it must be difficult with everything changing all the time, having power in some situations and no power in others.

Still she's not interested, telling me now about her friends and how she can't trust them; about how bitchy they can be, saying things behind people's backs.

I listen, but this feels too easy, all this talk of foolish teachers and treacherous friends. They're soft targets. 'Tell me about your mum, Laura.'

'What about my mum?'

'What's she like? What's she like to live with?'

'All right.'

'Go on...'

'I don't know,' she shrugs. 'What do you want to know?'

One of the difficult things about being a thirteen-year-old girl is making sense of a mother: old enough to be aware of her imperfections while young enough to need her to be perfect nonetheless; separating from her while still being merged; independent of her while still dependent. Freud's (1923) idea of an 'ego-ideal' is the sense of ourselves introjected from parents and others, an idealized self to which we aspire and about which we feel ashamed when we fall short. Like every young person, Laura is dealing with the ways in which she'll never be able to live up to an ideal of herself. All at once, she's dealing with a body that's changing in ways she can't control; she's dealing with menstruation, siblings, silly boys, homework deadlines, friendships, responsibilities at home, demands at school, PE lessons, Facebook... The list is endless. Everything's in flux. Most thirteen-year-old girls look to their mothers as a way of understanding themselves. 'In what ways am I like her? In what ways am I different? In what ways do I *want* to be like her and different from her? How do I understand her life and, by extension, my own?' In a sense, a mother is both a teacher and a friend, the two species that preoccupy and vex Laura.

'What's she like?'

'I don't know! You asked me that before.'

'Well, what does she look like?'

'Old,' says Laura. 'Saggy. Trying to be young. She actually wears my clothes sometimes. I mean, how sad is that!'

'What was she like when she was younger?'

'How should I know?' says Laura. 'I wasn't around!'

'She met your dad when they were teenagers... When they were both at school?'

She doesn't know. 'I think they'd left school. I think they might have met in a pub. He was with his mates – or something like that – and she was in there having a drink... Something like that. I don't know.'

'Was she in the pub with her own friends? Or waiting for someone? Or escaping from her family at home...?'

This is the easy bit, hearing her story and wondering about it together, wondering about people's motives, wondering about what her mother and father might have been like in those days, what they saw in each other, what they hoped for and what they found. Laura's sense of herself will depend considerably on the story she tells about her mother and father. Who they were and how they met are the first chapters in her autobiography. Teasing this out is important but relatively straightforward work. The harder work will be wondering about her mother *since* those days. What's she like now, this woman with four children by three different men and living now with a much younger man? What matters to her nowadays? And how exactly does Laura matter to this person who is both her teacher and friend? The stories Laura tells about teachers centre on their incomprehension and unfairness towards her. The stories she tells about friends are about betrayal, especially betrayals involving boys, and about inconsistencies: people saying one thing and doing another.

'It must have been difficult for you, Laura, getting used to all the changes at home over the years.'

'Not really,' she says. 'I just get on with my life. It's my mum's business what she does with hers.'

'But I imagine that you're expected to cope,' I say, 'to take responsibility for the little ones and not complain too much...'

'I suppose.'

'And you probably *do* do all that stuff, but people won't necessarily realize what it's been like for you.'

She looks at me as if to say, 'How did you know?'

Chodorow (1978) argues that a girl's sense of herself is embedded in her relationship with her mother; that mothers and daughters can easily identify with each other whereas mothers find it much harder to identify with their sons. If this is so, then I wonder about the extent to which Laura, identified with her mother, is likely to make similar choices in her life. Or, indeed, is likely to make radically different choices simply in order to separate from her mother.

I ask how her parents came to split up and she tells me about her father not doing anything around the house, her mother getting fed up and the two of them arguing. 'Then she met Mike. That's Stevie's dad. But he gambled and so she kicked him out. And when she found out she was pregnant, he still didn't want to know. So Stevie doesn't know his own dad.'

'And by now you were at primary school?'

'Yeah. And then she got with Dave who was all right. But then they started having arguments and they were both drinking a lot, so he left. We still see him and he still comes round sometimes to see Tyler.'

'And to see you and Jessie and Stevie?'

'Yeah, but he's got a girlfriend now and she's got kids of her own. So he doesn't come round so often because his girlfriend doesn't like it.'

I ask if she misses Dave.

'Not really. To be honest, most of the time I'm out of the house anyway.'

'And now your mum's with Simon?'

'Sounds bad, doesn't it,' says Laura. 'Like she's a slag or something.'

I ask Laura what she makes of it all. 'I guess it must be hard for your mum, having four kids…'

'It's her life,' Laura shrugs. 'No one told her to get pregnant. It's up to her, really.'

I ask whether her mum gets lonely, whether her mum's parents are still around, whether her mum works or wants to work.

In all this, our conversation is really about Laura, about her life and future through the lens of her mother's story.

I suggest that her mother might have felt let down, betrayed by the men in her life.

She nods. 'Mum complains all the time, but you can tell she can't wait to have another bloke. After Simon, there's bound to be someone else!'

'Because?'

'Because she's like that,' says Laura. 'She's got to have a man!'

'Because she's not really so confident?'

'Probably… I know she does regret things. She says she doesn't regret having us, but you can tell she regrets us having different dads.'

We pause.

'Maybe the sex is sometimes important to people as well?'

Laura looks uneasy. 'Shouldn't be important, though, should it!'

'Well, maybe people need the closeness,' I suggest. 'Maybe it makes people feel wanted.'

'It's still not a good enough reason to get with someone,' says Laura. 'And if you're going to do it, at least use protection!'

Although she's only thirteen, it's important to bring the word 'sex' into our conversation, if only to establish it as one of the many things we might choose to talk about. Sex weighs heavily in the minds of most young people as something waiting further up the road, exotic but scary, impossible to ignore. Between themselves, girls might talk about sex a lot, but it's much harder to talk about sex with adults (and male counsellors). And it's especially hard to talk about the sexuality of one's parents. At a time when Laura's becoming aware of her own capacity to be sexual, she's obliged to live with her mother's overt neediness. 'Women seek directly to reconstitute, resurrect, re-shape, reimagine an emotional relation with their mothers,' writes Chodorow (1994). 'They fantasize and unconsciously experience internal and actual mothers even as they form relationships with men' (p.82). Laura and I go on to speculate about whether her mother wanted babies more than she wanted a boyfriend and whether she wanted babies because she needed people to love and to love her. Still we're always talking about Laura by extension: about her own needs, values and dilemmas. We're thinking these things through together, puzzling them out, coming to no conclusions but giving her the chance to think with another person rather than sit in a room by herself, tormented by possibilities, taking it out on her arms and on various people at school.

'I wonder if your life will be different from your mum's, Laura?'

'Shouldn't think so,' she says. Then changes her mind. 'Yeah, I'm not going to do all the stuff my mum's done. I'm going to have a life before I start having kids. I'm going to wait until I'm at least – I don't know – twenty-two or twenty-three before I have any.'

'Until you meet someone who really loves you for who you are …'

'Yeah!'

We pause.

'How will you know?'

'Know what?'

'Know whether the person really loves you? It's hard to be sure. People make promises sometimes and then break them.'

'Tell me about it!' she says wearily. 'That's what always happens with my mum. That's why I'm going to wait before I have kids. I want them to have a proper dad.'

'And you to have a proper lover …'

'Yeah, not someone who fucks off as soon as he's got what he wants!'

We continue to talk and continue to meet, thinking about her life now and in the future, thinking about the uncertainty of everything – the disappointments, the resolutions and mistakes we make, the lessons we learn, the mother she has and the woman Laura might become. Whereas Chodorow (1978) suggests that the identities of a mother and her daughter are entwined, Orbach and Eichenbaum (1994) take a less benign view, arguing that girls are essentially alone:

> Girls learn early on [from their mothers] that in the most profound sense they must rely on themselves, that there

is no one to take care of them emotionally. They cannot assume – as does the man – that there will be someone for them to bring their emotional lives to. (p.11)

Consciously or unconsciously, it's easy for young people to find themselves re-creating relationships internalized from their parents, finding a partner and then copying that original template. I've known daughters who effectively become their mothers, but I've also known daughters who don't. For many young people, sexual relationships are opportunities to do things differently. Some young people are determined not to repeat their parents' mistakes, determined to behave differently, yet at the same time, they're caught up in developmental processes over which they have little or no control.

Like Laura, Ellis is also trying to make sense of himself in relation to a mother. He comes to see me of his own accord but with the strong encouragement of teachers because he's been caught watching porn on his phone during a lesson in school. His mother has been told and is appalled. So my official job is to Stop Ellis Watching Porn.

I meet with a very likeable fourteen-year-old boy who's confused.

'Everyone else watches it, so I don't see what's so wrong!'

I agree with him that most boys watch porn and some boys watch lots of porn. We have a short conversation about porn being unrealistic, about the bad attitude of most porn towards women, and about good sex being loving sex. But porn itself was never going to be the real issue.

'She thinks I'm a child! She expects me to be in bed by nine o'clock on schooldays and she wants to know what I'm doing every minute of the day!'

Ellis lives alone with his mother who, from time to time, has boyfriends. None of these relationships lasts very long. His father lives elsewhere with a new partner and young sons, but because his mother and father are still at war, Ellis rarely sees his father or half-brothers.

'My dad agrees with me that it's stupid! I speak to him on the phone sometimes – when she lets me – and he says he thinks I should be allowed to stay up later and have more freedom. He agrees with me!'

Counsellors have to be careful about suggesting things to young people because most of those young people live with at least one parent and have little power to change the world or the parent they might find so annoying. A strict nine o'clock bedtime does sound inappropriate for a fourteen-year-old but saying this to Ellis would risk antagonizing his mother ('And what's more, Mum, my counsellor agrees with me that nine o'clock is far too early!') and would risk his mother insisting that he stop meeting with me ('Well, that's the last time you'll be seeing the counsellor then!'). There are more important things at stake than bedtimes. How can I help Ellis feel more confident in a relationship with his mother fraught with confusions of sexuality? How can he begin to make sense of their relationship when her boyfriends come and go, when his role as her consort is usurped and then reinstated, when the Oedipal triumph of having his mother to himself has come without a fight and when he's right in the middle of puberty, probably masturbating guiltily in his room next to the one where his mother lies alone most nights?

A lot is at stake. I've known boys in Ellis's position who, feeling powerless and afraid at the same time as they're becoming bigger and stronger, resort to violence in order to establish their physical power at home and in order to separate from their mothers. Jukes (1993) claims that this experience is at the heart of misogyny. I've known boys who behave in sexually inappropriate ways, fuelled by pornographic fantasies of male potency and muddled by a confusion of sexual boundaries at home. (I haven't yet asked Ellis about the privacy protocols when one of his mother's boyfriends is staying.) In any situation involving young people, there are always developmental processes being played out. Like any boy separating from his parents, Ellis might love and hate the world and, like any boy, might look to split his parents into the good one and the bad one (Luxmoore 2010). With a 'good' father on the phone, agreeing with his opinions about bedtimes, Ellis's mother easily becomes the wicked witch against whom Ellis rages, hating his need for her and hating her for causing that neediness. As Winnicott (1965) describes, the hating child quickly becomes the guilty child unless there are opportunities for him to make amends for his hating. Without such opportunities, the danger is that Ellis, like other boys, ends up taking his guilt out on himself or on other people: fighting with himself or fighting with parent-figures at school and, little by little, convincing himself that he really is a bad person for behaving in these ways, that he's a person condemned to a lifetime of badness.

I could talk to Ellis about all this, warning him of the dangers I foresee. He might understand but, in the heat of the moment, his anxiety would always get the better of him. He'd still end up lashing out and then regretting it afterwards. If I can help him to feel less anxious, less guilty inside, then his external world – his behaviour – will take care of itself. His internal world is my priority.

I ask what it's like when his mother has boyfriends.

He's surprisingly enthusiastic. 'We play computer games sometimes, which is cool. And watch films. Not just the boring ones my mum wants me to watch but adventure films, action stuff.'

This makes sense. With another man in the house, Ellis is relieved of the terrible intimacy of being alone with his mother. Perhaps he feels better able to get on with his own sex life, knowing that she's getting on with hers.

I ask what it's like when she splits up with a boyfriend.

'Boring, because I know I'm never going to see him again. It's just back to the same old thing.'

'Which gets embarrassing?'

He nods vigorously. 'Yeah, it is embarrassing. Like when she's in the bath or something or when she's walking round the house with nothing on! I hate that!'

If most boys compete with their fathers for their mothers' affections, Ellis has won that Oedipal battle without a fight. He has his mother to himself: every boy's dream but also every boy's dread, knowing that he can't do anything with the situation because he's too young and because he's her son, not her lover. How much better if a mother has a boyfriend for a son to hate ('How dare you sleep with my mum!'), someone who can be what Ellis can't be, who can relieve him of feelings of sexual inadequacy, feelings compounded by a mother who treats him like a child?

We talk together about power and powerlessness, about standing up to his mother sometimes and giving way to her at other times.

'I imagine that it gets annoying,' I say, 'now that you're getting older and taller and stronger all the time? Now that you can do things for yourself?'

'Yeah, *really* annoying!'

I assure him that it really *is* a tough situation. 'It may not be your mum's fault and it may not be your fault, but it's a hard situation for both of you.'

Wanting to acknowledge his masculinity, I joke about shaving. 'You're getting a bit of moustache, Ellis!'

He looks pleased. He says his mother doesn't want him to start shaving because she thinks that it'll make the stubble grow more quickly.

I ask if he knows how to shave. He doesn't. I describe the various processes. He's very interested in this and, by the time we meet again, has not only persuaded his mother to buy him his own razor but has had his first shave. (I wonder to myself whether 'My counsellor agrees with me!' might have been used as leverage.) He's delighted with himself, stroking his cheeks like a veteran. When I commiserate about the lifetime of shaving now ahead of him, he says he doesn't mind, clearly proud to have entered a man's world separating him from his mother. When I ask about his current porn consumption, he says he's been watching less, which I don't entirely believe. When I mention masturbating, he says he's been taking my advice and only doing it behind locked doors or when his mother is out of the house…

My intention is to detoxify his superego: that voice telling him that he's bad, ungrateful, disobedient and unloving. In a sense, I'm suggesting to him that being angry with his mother is normal, being embarrassed about her is normal, hating her is normal, watching porn and masturbating are normal things to do. None of these things mean that he isn't *also* a kind, loving, protective, loyal son.

Over time he becomes more relaxed, less angry. He's still keen to tell me about his annoying mother but often with an ironic smile, as if having a mother is really no more than an occupational hazard for an independent, fourteen-year-old boy. And we begin to talk more about his father, wondering whether his father has an easy life in many ways: keeping out of the way and agreeing with whatever Ellis says.

If all behaviour is an unconscious communication of some sort, I wonder about the behaviour that got Ellis into trouble in the first place. He'd deny it, but I wonder whether there was unconscious method in being caught watching porn. I wonder whether he found a way of drawing attention to himself, as if he was effectively saying to the world, 'I'm in a muddle about things to do with sexuality: about whether I should have any power over other people, especially over my mum, and whether I want any power anyway. It's frightening, especially when it comes to sex. I don't know what to do! Tell me what to do! I hate being a child, but at the same time, I wish I didn't have to grow up!'

Winnicott (1965) famously suggests that parents should strive to be 'good enough', freeing themselves from the tyranny of success or failure. For Ellis, as for many young people, the task is to be a good-enough son: neither a winner nor a loser but necessarily imperfect, forgivably imperfect, loveably imperfect.

There are young people for whom there can be no such thing as 'good enough' sex, however. The sex they experience is never as extravagant as on the porn sites; the other person is never as seductive and rarely behaves like the actors and actresses. I think that, having been necessarily disappointed by their parents, many young people spend a lot of time looking for replacements who *will* be perfect. So when the latest replacement turns out to be imperfect in bed, the temptation is to split up immediately ('We're obviously not right for each other because the sex is no better than average!'), which many young people do, hurting each other in the process. For many, sex (like 'getting a job' and 'going to university') is occasionally great but usually ends up as a bit of a disappointment and beneath all disappointments is an original disappointment with a parent.

Tayla's dad is one such disappointment. She doesn't see much of him: once or twice a year when he's back in the country before he's off again, leaving her to decide whether or not to bother with the relationship, whether to say, 'That's it! I never want to see you again!' or to persist despite the disappointments, the broken promises, the sense of things never being as good as they could be.

'I know I don't matter to him as much as Jack,' she says, 'and that's all right. I don't mind because Jack lives with Dad and sees him every day. That's fair enough. Dad's bound to be more interested in Jack.'

Jack is Tayla's half-brother. When she was three, her father left Tayla and her mum and went to live with his girlfriend – now wife – in Spain. They had Jack – their only child – when Tayla was eight.

Tayla's mum remarried a man Tayla likes. 'But he's not my dad,' she says imploringly. 'It would just be nice – when I do see my dad – for him to be a bit interested in what I'm doing. And ask me a few things.' She smiles but her smile is almost a wince, bittersweet and hurting. Tayla is old enough to understand that couples split up and that it's sometimes for the best; she understands that parents are entitled to their new lives and that with new partners come new children. Sometimes. She gets all that. What she doesn't get is her father's behaviour towards her and what sense to make of it. Does he love her? Think about her? Care about her? Or is she a burden to him, the needy legacy of a failed relationship, a reminder of a time he'd rather forget?

A girl's need for a father never goes away, despite the most painful setbacks. A girl might come downstairs in a new top and short skirt, ready to go out with friends, feeling worried about how she looks but hoping that she looks glamorous, hoping that her father will approve, sending her out into the evening with a reminder that she looks lovely, beautiful, attractive. She might instead be told that she looks like a whore, a slag, like she's begging for sex and that no daughter of his is going to leave the house looking like that.

Some fathers don't realize how crushing this feels for a daughter when the man she first looked to for approval rejects her best teenage efforts to look good. Fathers are jealous, scared that their daughter has reached an age when she's ready to make relationships and potentially sexual relationships with other males. Boys become instant threats to the paternal empire, to be ridiculed and despised simply because they're there, waiting outside the school gates or waiting outside the house: waiting, always waiting, never going away.

Some daughters retaliate with their own withering scorn ('You're not a proper dad! You don't understand anything! You're an embarrassment!'). They stop speaking to their fathers. Other daughters retreat, wounded, to the shelter of their rooms, defeated or taking stock, deciding how best to circumvent so hurtful an obstacle.

Tayla does neither of these things because her father has never reacted to her in such a heavy-handed way. He's simply been absent: physically absent for most of her life and emotionally absent on the rare occasions when the two of them are together.

'He's always checking his phone when I'm talking,' she says, 'and I know perfectly well that he's not listening. He's texting other people or seeing if he's got any messages.'

This story informs all her stories. Without making the connection, she's forever telling me about friends who are distracted, about relatives who take her for granted, about teachers who seem more interested in other students despite Tayla's best attempts to do well at school, to try hard, to ingratiate herself. She tells me these stories, mystified and furious, indignant and saddened by other people's behaviour.

'Maybe he's just not good at being a dad,' I say to her. 'Maybe he's got his own needs and can't understand that other people might also be needing things from him ...'

She thinks about this. 'That's no excuse, though, is it! I'm not asking for much! I'm only asking for him to pay me a little bit of attention sometimes!'

I feel for her. 'You're right, Tayla. You're not asking for much. And yet he can't seem to do it.'

There's silence between us.

'I guess he's the dad you've got. He may not be the one you need. And he may not be the one you deserve. But he's the one you've got.'

More silence.

'And I guess that's what you can't change. What none of us can change about our parents.'

She's angry now, a child inside her fifteen-year-old body. 'But it's not fair!'

'I know it's not, Tayla. I know.'

I let her cry.

'And maybe your dad will never realize what a kind, strong, talented daughter he's got. Maybe that'll always be sad. But it won't stop you getting on with your life. It won't stop you loving other people and being loved by them.'

Our work isn't done. The danger is that, having internalized this relationship with an absent father, she'll replace him with other relationships also characterized by absence and disappointment, replaying the story of this first, formative relationship, as if she expects and deserves no better. In future sessions we'll think more about her father, about the years before Tayla was born and the years immediately afterwards, the years leading up to the split. We'll wonder about these things together, always acknowledging her need for a father but also acknowledging and trying to understand the story of this particular man, flawed like the rest of us, but also, like the rest of us, unlikely to change.

In all this, her relationship with the father-figure sitting across from her in the counselling room will be important…

8

SEXUALITY IN THE COUNSELLING ROOM

TWO PEOPLE MEET. They're alone in a room. They spend a lot of time looking at each other. At times, they can even smell each other. They talk about very personal things and inevitably, because they're people, they develop strong feelings about each other.

In any relationship where one person confides in another, trusting in that person, at times tearful, at times joyful, at times despairing, the trusted confidante (unless she or he deliberately refuses any emotional contact) is likely to feel strongly towards the person confiding. The confidante might well feel physically drawn to the other person, if only in wanting to hug the distressed person or to offer the reassurance of a hand placed tenderly on a shoulder.

Feeling these things is very different from enacting them. But acknowledging our fondness, our protectiveness or admiration for the other person in the room doesn't make us more likely to enact these feelings. Rather the opposite. Acknowledging these feelings to ourselves and to our supervisors helps us to think about and control any temptation to act them out, reducing the potential for abuse (Spinelli 1994).

Young people come to counselling anxious about whether or not their counsellor will like and approve of them. Never knowing what the counsellor thinks potentially causes a young person to regress to the uncertainties and anxieties of infancy. 'Does my mother like me? Does my father approve of me?' Some counsellors might argue that such regression allows the young person now to experience these anxieties differently, understanding that life really *is* tough and that parental love *can't* be bought with a smile or an achievement or a bit of coercion. The trouble is that needy young people aren't going to stick around, putting up with months of anxious wondering about what their counsellor really thinks in order to 'work through' their anxieties. They'll be gone and won't come back!

A counsellor has to communicate a liking and approval of the young person (whatever that young person's mistakes or shortcomings) in order for therapy to be sustained and for the young person to keep coming back. I don't mean gushing, desperate flattery but warmth, kindness and enthusiasm, an obvious interest in the young person from week to week, an appreciation of his or her presence. Most young people come to counselling feeling battered and bruised, feeling badly about themselves and antagonistic towards other people. When they discover in their counsellor's eyes not condemnation and despair but admiration and delight, a therapeutic process becomes possible. 'The crying baby asks for comfort,' writes Alvarez (2012), while 'the smiling and performing baby asks for something like delight, to bring a light to someone's eyes' (p.127). If no one delights in the baby, then it never learns to delight in itself or in anyone else. When the parent delights in the baby and, years later, the lover delights in the beloved, the world becomes a different place, full of new possibilities, new ways of being. Counsellors will also delight in young people, however miserable or blank a young person might look; counsellors will laugh when things are funny; they'll be interested and keen to understand; sometimes they'll say how much they admire a young person's qualities.

Sexuality can never be dismissed from the counselling room because sexuality is at the heart of admiration and delight, of warmth and kindness, of playfulness, of laughter that's spontaneous. In fact, counselling conversations always mirror a kind of sexual exchange with two people struggling to get started, trying to read each other; one partner sometimes feeling that he or she is making all the running; both partners negotiating power and powerlessness, control and surrender, working hard to remain in tune with each other...

I sometimes wonder what it would be like for a young person to have counselling with an ageing Nelson Mandela or Mother Teresa. What would be gained and what would be lost? Presumably there'd be lots of wisdom in the room. Lots of understanding and forgiveness. Lots of calm. But what would happen to the sexuality? Would it lose its edge, its danger? Would it be kept under wraps? And would that be a relief or a frustration for the young person? What would it be like if, instead of Nelson Mandela or Mother Teresa, the door opened and the counsellor turned out to be a glamorous pop star or muscular sportsperson? Then what would be lost and what would be gained?

Of course it depends what we mean by 'sexuality'. As I said in the introduction to this book, I mean 'sexuality' in the broadest sense: the fondness we feel for each other, the ways in which we find each other attractive, the ways in which we like or dislike each other's company. Genital sexuality has a much narrower focus, and yet our attraction towards other people will always be somewhere on a continuum between an urgent desire for sexual intercourse at one extreme and a completely platonic admiration at the other. It would be so much easier if these ends of the continuum could be kept separate. Counsellors could say to themselves, 'Phew, I don't want to have sexual intercourse with this young person, so sexuality isn't an issue between us! I'm not allowing any of that erotic transference and counter-transference into *my* counselling room!' It would be easier but it would be an avoidance, because things are never so straightforward (Page 1999; Yalom 1996). Counsellors always get stuck when they're unable to or refuse to think about what's going on between the two people sitting together in the room, looking at each other, looking away, looking back again.

I sit with fifteen-year-old Tiffany, for example. I think she's very beautiful and imagine that, if I was also fifteen years old, I'd want to get to know her, I'd want her to like me, I'd probably want to have sex with her. I feel nostalgic for those days: happy for her that she's so beautiful and sad for myself that those days are gone. I say nothing about this to Tiffany, who'd be horrified to know that some old counsellor found her attractive!

She's talking to me about her father and about his lack of interest in her life, so perhaps what I'm feeling is related to him. Perhaps I want to make up for his neglect. 'I could love you, Tiffany!' I catch myself thinking. 'I could be your dad!' I'm alarmed and vaguely ashamed that a fifteen-year-old girl excites these feelings in me. I can now unwittingly punish Tiffany for being so desirable by concentrating solely on her words and by ignoring everything else about her. And perhaps that's what happens with her father. Perhaps he gets scared of his feelings for his beautiful daughter and shuns her as the only way he knows of dealing with his feelings. Yet Tiffany *wants* to be desired – that's the point of our conversation about her father. She complains that he never says anything nice to her, won't look her in the eye and won't go anywhere near her. Wanting to be desired by him doesn't mean that she wants her father or anyone else to have sex with her. It means that she wants him to find her attractive, to have that affirmation, safe in the knowledge that he *won't* want to have sex with her.

That said, there's a potentially uncomfortable overlap between the desire felt by a parent or parent-figure (such as a counsellor) and the desire felt by a lover. Both the parent and the lover want to hold their beloved tight. For the parent, that's enough, whereas for the lover, it's not.

My role as her counsellor is to affirm and enjoy Tiffany's beauty without fear and without spurning or shaming her. She's beautiful and I'm glad. I'm not intending to have sex with her and would never abuse her trust. I have nothing to be ashamed of. I do think that she's beautiful, though, but as her counsellor, I'd never say that to her, whereas a real father might quite appropriately tell his daughter that she's beautiful. I imagine that Tiffany will sense my admiration all the same, without me needing to say anything. I share Luca's (2015) view that:

> the [therapist's] erotic, loving feelings are potentially transformational for the client. Many of our clients harbour the desire to have an impact on us: to influence us, to challenge us and penetrate through us in their attempt to know us and be special to us. If we conceive of the therapy relationship as one of reciprocal mutual influence, we become aware that intersubjectively clients

and therapists have mutual insights. Our clients have intuitive perceptions about us; just as we tune into them, they sense us. (p.19)

If this is right, if all clients want to be special to their counsellors, and if all counsellors want to be special to their clients, then one of the ways in which we manage these secret desires is by keeping the boundaries of our sessions consistent: we start and we finish on time; we make no special allowances. These practical boundaries are helpful, but trying to put boundaries around the *quality* of our interactions ('I won't smile or laugh, I'll never say anything about myself...') is less helpful, especially when it'll be the quality of these interactions that most helps young people.

I see Tiffany a month or so after we've finished meeting. She's sitting on a bench with her back to me, leaning forward, chatting with a boy, something I've never seen her doing before, at least not chatting in *that* way. I feel a pang of jealousy, then pride. Good for you, Tiffany, I think to myself. Good for you.

When we're scared to acknowledge the sexuality in the counselling room (and scared of asking young people about sex) it's usually because we're afraid that some latent genital feeling will be activated and will overtake us. The 'Lolita' debate still rages. Is it normal or perverse for an adult to find a young person sexually attractive? For most counsellors it's shaming to admit to being attracted to a young person, but I think that sexual attraction (or repulsion) in the broadest sense is inevitable in all professional relationships, especially where intimacy and trust are central to the working relationship. It's the same with priests. It's the same with doctors. It's the same with teachers. 'The difficulty of achieving safe therapy, like safe sex,' writes Murdin (2000), 'is that there is no such thing' (p.67).

In my experience, there are counsellors who get frightened and retreat from their sexual feelings towards clients, feeling ashamed, especially if the other person in the room is young. Once upon a time in psychoanalytic circles it was thought that a client's erotic transference to the analyst was a resistance (Freud 1915), a way of unconsciously diverting attention away from more important issues. And it was thought that an analyst's erotic *counter*-transference was a failure on the analyst's part requiring further analysis in order to rid the analyst of such human frailty. More recently, Gabbard and Twernlow (1989) are scathing about 'lovestruck' therapists, attributing the lovesickness, if not to the therapist's anti-social or psychotic tendencies, then to defects in the therapist's superego, to narcissistic disturbances or to the therapist's failure to resolve his or her own Oedipal conflicts. Nowadays counsellors still blame themselves for having erotic feelings about young people. They might decide to go back into therapy themselves in order to try and deal with this unforeseen, uncomfortable experience, or they might blame the young person, interpreting his or her unabashed sexuality as just another kind of defence needing to be confronted.

Sitting alone with a young person and aware that these feelings are present in the room, counsellors can live in fear or they can accept such feelings as inevitable, engaging in ways that help rather than hinder a young person's growth, allowing delight, playfulness, humour and admiration into the therapeutic relationship, approaching that relationship as a collaboration, confident that no ethical boundaries will be broken, confident enough to acknowledge that sexuality is everywhere and therefore unavoidable. 'In my view,' writes Luca (2015), 'the threat of inappropriate enactment is more pertinent if therapists ignore erotic feelings in their clients and in themselves' (p.20). Staunton (2002) argues that:

> The therapist 'being available' has a meaning beyond attentiveness, active listening and therapeutic presence. It means that, as therapist, I can be reached: I can feel attracted, bathed, soothed, stimulated or aroused by the client. I can also feel repelled and disgusted, or feel a total lack of erotic interest. (p.68)

These things matter. The therapist and young person have to attach, to make a 'therapeutic alliance' in order to continue working productively. Sexuality will always play a part in that attachment.

So when a therapeutic alliance doesn't seem possible and a young person finishes counselling prematurely, it's tempting for counsellors to blame themselves: 'I couldn't feel close to him... I couldn't get close to her...' This is much easier to admit than 'I felt *very* close to him...' or 'I felt *powerfully* drawn to her...' I know that it can be genuinely hard to attach to someone who's smelly, who's monosyllabic or can't concentrate, who's physically unattractive or repulsive. Counselling relationships sometimes end for these reasons. It's just that sometimes the therapeutic rupture occurs, *not* because of the counsellor's failure to connect, but because of the feeling of absolute connectedness in the room. Both people get scared. Young people are perfectly well aware of the sexuality of the relationship, even if they can't name it. So unless the counsellor can find a way forward, some young people, unnerved, will finish counselling as quickly as possible, reporting vaguely that 'I just couldn't get on with my counsellor'. Counsellors have to be aware, not only of their own feelings towards the young person, but also of how they might be coming across to that young person. What is it about themselves that helps or hinders the therapeutic alliance?

Lucas and I were together in our supervision meeting, trying to understand what made fifteen-year-old Elodie decide to end her counselling meetings with him. She'd recently split up with her much older boyfriend, which may have had some bearing on things, but she'd been reluctant to meet with Lucas long before that, needing to be fetched from classrooms and, finally, sending messages through her teachers to say that she no longer wanted to see him.

Lucas was a good counsellor, a thoughtful and honest counsellor. He was also a counsellor with straggly dreadlocks and a wild blond beard he never bothered to trim. Despite wearing conventional clothes for work, he still managed to look like a hippie. I imagined Elodie's friends saying to her, 'Are you going to see that bloke? The weird one?' and I imagined her feeling embarrassed because, however much she may have felt appreciated by Lucas, he probably did look weird to her and his appearance probably was hard to see past.

Struggling to understand and not quite sure of the implications of my question, I asked, 'Was it sexual, Lucas?'

Immediately he asked what I meant. But explaining was difficult. I was embarrassed, afraid of hurting someone whose dreadlocks and beard probably meant a lot to him. Commenting on my supervisee's physical appearance seemed entirely unfair, but I ploughed on, hoping that he'd cope with what I was trying to say but worrying all the while in case I was saying more about myself and about my own response to his appearance than about Elodie and whatever might have been going on between the two of them.

'Some girls have a strong sense of how men look,' I said, clumsily. 'They're keen on men with slick haircuts, on fashionable townie-boys. By "sexual", I don't mean "Did Elodie want to have sex with you?", but I was wondering how comfortable she might have felt with you, physically?'

I squirmed.

'Are you saying that I'm different from what she's used to?'

That's it, I thought, happy to argue that, in homogeneous schools, it's important to promote difference, but that if a counsellor is *too* different it potentially jeopardizes the relationship. I knew that some young people in school jokingly referred to Lucas as 'Gandalf' and I'd heard him called ruder names behind his back. But still I was on shaky ground. If Lucas was black and Elodie was white, would that be too different? Of course not! If he was gay and she was straight, would that be too different? Certainly not! So what exactly *was* I saying?

I once supervised a counsellor who wore black all the time. He was well built and wore his black clothes very tightly with shirt buttons undone at the top so that his chest hair was visible. There were tattoos on his arms and, typically, he sat with his legs apart, the outline of his balls visible inside tight black trousers.

I remember saying to him that it might be hard for a thirteen-year-old girl to relax, alone in a room with him and obliged to sit opposite such a frightening sight! I said that he needed to think about his appearance because appearances do matter in counselling and he'd lose young people if they couldn't relax with him.

He could have said that appearances shouldn't matter, that he was being himself and was entitled to wear whatever he wanted. He could have said that unless I was prepared to ask his clients what *they* thought, I was probably only voicing some prejudice of my own about black clothes and expressing my own jealousy of his physique. (I *was* jealous!) Fortunately, he didn't say any of these things and we were able to talk more interestingly.

I think that we can't help noticing and reacting to the physical appearance of the other person. After all, we sit there with *all* of the other person: not only with her words and internal life, but also with her clothes, colours, hairstyle, smell, the sound of her voice, the way her body shifts in the chair.

In counselling with young people, difficulties arise when the erotic transference between client and counsellor becomes idealized or demonized, when we fancy the other person or find the other person repugnant. Our reaction will probably be informed by earlier relationships in our lives and by all sorts of unconscious processes, which is why erotic transference needs to be a regular topic of conversation in supervision. But our reaction to the person will also be informed by objective as well as subjective experience, and that's why Lucas's appearance seemed worth discussing.

As I've said, effective counselling with young people requires a benign attraction to the other person, and that attraction can take many forms. We might find the other person intellectually or emotionally attractive. We might enjoy their humour. We might find them physically attractive in a way that's unthreatening, unarousing and yet enjoyable in the way that a parent finds his or her child physically attractive. Schwartz (2007) believes that 'In cases where strong erotic feelings are present in the consulting room it is essential to be able to enjoy erotic feelings in the countertransference without conflict or need' (p.52). If the erotic transference and countertransference are idealized (we fancy the other person) or demonized (we find them repulsive), it'll be too dangerous for sexuality to become part of the conversation for fear that these feelings will be acted out in some way. The subject of sexuality will be sublimated, avoided at all costs by the two people in the room. Yet it'll always be there.

And that was the issue for Lucas. Elodie had just split up from her older boyfriend with whom she was probably having a sexual relationship. It might have been her first sexual relationship. It would be hard for a fifteen-year-old girl to talk with her counsellor about this at the best of times (assuming she wanted to) but impossible if there was a sexual uneasiness between them.

Young people only talk about the things and only talk at the level that they think their counsellor can bear. If they sense a physical or sexual unease in the counsellor, they'll avoid the topic of sex and sexuality. If the counsellor determinedly offers a blank, asexual response to a young person, then the young person will become blank and asexual, at least in the counselling room. I imagine that for Elodie, as for most fifteen-year-old young people, how she looked and whether or not she felt sexually attractive was a hugely important part of her life. But it would have felt impossible to talk to Lucas about this if she felt that he looked strange or seemed uneasy in his own body. And he *did* look uneasy, his conventional shirt and tie at odds with his straggly dreadlocks and wild blond beard. He was younger than his old man's beard made him look, tugging at a stray lock of hair and tucking it behind his ear as if he was anxious about something.

In choosing a counsellor, we probably look for people who are like ourselves in some way, imagining – rightly or wrongly – that we'll be able to attach to these people, that they'll keep us safe and understand us. Staunton (2002) identifies a 'somatic' kind of transference and countertransference in therapy, an awareness of the physicality of the other person, while Holmes (2010) proposes the notion of 'hedonic intersubjectivity… a playful, self-affirming, interactive sensuality' (p.99) between the two people in the room. I think of fifteen-year-old Tiffany and wonder whether her transference to me was to a father who would notice and admire her. Perhaps I became the transferential father she needed, enjoying the sensuality of our relationship without acting anything out.

Of course, a counsellor's physical appearance isn't the only thing that we take into account in making our choice. We look for other identifications as well, for a rapport that can become a therapeutic alliance. But how the counsellor looks is certainly *one* of the factors that we take into account. And if the counsellor looks odd in some way, then that's not necessarily the end of the relationship because, so long as the counsellor seems comfortable in his or her oddness, we can relax. A counsellor might be sporting a bright green Mohican haircut: that in itself matters less than our sense of the counsellor's ease or unease with the haircut. A Mohican haircut exuding anger is likely to disconcert. A Mohican somehow expressing a counsellor's need to be noticed is likely to leave clients feeling anxious.

Would Elodie have felt better able to talk about sex and sexuality with a female counsellor? Possibly, but gender is only one of many factors when it comes to choosing a counsellor, and female counsellors are just as capable of disconcerting girls with their appearance. I've supervised excellent female counsellors who've lost girl clients because something made the girl uneasy: the counsellor's vocabulary perhaps, or reticence, or low-cut top, or choice of clothes. Inevitably, there will be unconscious factors at play: a female counsellor might look more like a mother than a father and Elodie might have all sorts of reasons to mistrust mothers. But appearances will also be important. An obese counsellor might find herself working with an anorexic girl. A pregnant counsellor might find herself working with a girl who's had an abortion. Another counsellor's wedding ring might be significant, or her piercings, or her sudden change of hairstyle. None of these things mean that the relationship is necessarily doomed, but they'll almost certainly need to be acknowledged and thought about. They'll matter.

'How do I look?' isn't a question that we ask our supervisors. But perhaps we should. Robust, honest feedback might tell us important things about ourselves and about our likely effect on young people. It was precisely this robust kind of feedback that I avoided giving Lucas. I could have said, 'Lucas, you look a mess! You look like someone pretending to be a counsellor. Your hair and beard are at odds with your conventional clothes and that makes you look *confusing*.' He might have hated me for saying this but could have taken it to his own therapy and thought about why someone might say these things. I think I'd have been doing him a favour if I'd had the courage to say what I was thinking.

The way we dress, the way we talk, the way we smile and greet a young person, the way we shift in our chairs as we think about things, the way we listen, frown, gesticulate… We can't stop our sexuality coming into the counselling room with us and we can't ask young people to leave their sexuality outside the room. We can try ignoring the sexuality in the room, regarding it as too dangerous to face, or we can find ways of engaging with it appropriately. The question is, what's 'appropriate' and what isn't? How exactly do we engage with sexuality in ways that are safe and supportive of the therapeutic process?

Following Freud's (1905) old idea that 'the symptoms constitute the sexual activity of the patient' (p.279), Mann (1997) goes so far as to suggest that 'the patient's way of relating in a psychotherapy session frequently mirrors how they relate during sexual intercourse...' (p.120). I find this idea compelling and slightly creepy. What's useful is the implication that there might be similarities between how a person relates in one context and in another, that we each carry a relational template and apply it to whatever context we're in. So a girl who's shy in the counselling room might be shy in the bedroom. A boy who's overbearing and controlling in a counselling relationship might behave similarly in a sexual relationship. Perhaps there's nothing very surprising about this, but it means that counselling is a context in which young people practise relationships, repeating old, familiar patterns or trying out new ones. And practising relationships is what counselling is often about. A young person who's never been able to excite the admiration of a parent will doubt his or her ability to excite the admiration of a lover or, indeed, of a counsellor. Old strategies will be tried. Old behaviours will probably produce the same old results. But in counselling, new strategies, new behaviours and new responses are possible in a relationship where it's safe enough to practise without being punished for making mistakes. Just as the playfulness between a mother and her baby is what allows the baby to try out new behaviours, so the playfulness in a counselling relationship is what allows the young person to practise new behaviours, new ways of being. 'Psychotherapy has to do with two people playing together,' writes Winnicott (1971, p.38).

But how can a counsellor be playful without becoming flirtatious? Bramley (2014) calls it 'foreplay' rather than flirtation. Therapeutic foreplay, she suggests, is as necessary for therapy as sexual foreplay is necessary for sex:

> Successful foreplay leads to a deeper trustful bond such that – all other things being equal – the pair will remain together... Foreplay is also about how to assist the partner to surrender control and control surrender (in other words be able to lose but find themselves again)... If therapeutic foreplay isn't forthcoming, patients may well 'freeze up' or just leave. (pp.16–17)

I agree with this. Flirting, as Alvarez (2012) observes, 'need not be seen as a purely seductive act. If it is occurring on the symbolic level, it can involve a type of playing, of acknowledging attraction, but under safe conditions' (p.121).

I think about this as I sit with thirteen-year-old Rohan. He takes a biro from his rucksack and, pulling out the ink cartridge, holds the empty outer tube of the biro in his hand. He removes a sheet of paper from his folder and starts tearing off bits of paper which, one at a time, he sucks, rolls between his forefinger and thumb and puts into the tube of the biro. Taking his time and aiming carefully, he blows sharply down the tube, firing a succession of soggy little paper bullets at the wall opposite.

I watch, wondering what happens next. But I know perfectly well what happens next. Rohan holds his biro-weapon and looks at me mischievously.

We've been working together for several months, talking about how his week has been, his friends and enemies, his continuing troubles in school. Whenever the time seems right, I ask about his mother at home, and typically he tells me that he and his mother have just had a massive row. On another occasion, he tells me that they're getting on really well, then that they've had a massive row, then that they're getting on really well. Occasionally we talk about his father who was violent and left after beating up Rohan's mother (not for the first time) when Rohan was three years old.

Sensing his reluctance to talk about this man of whom he has no conscious memory, I go slowly. Whenever we do manage a conversation about his father, Rohan becomes especially vituperative, vowing to kill his father if ever they meet. Therapeutically, I think we need to unpick the autobiographical story Rohan is telling, the one in which his mother is 'brilliant' one week and 'a bitch' the next, while his father and school are forever 'shit'. We need to work towards a more ambivalent view of the world if he's eventually to develop a more nuanced understanding of himself because, in the stories he tells at the moment, he's either good-boy Rohan or bad-boy Rohan. Nothing else. Nothing in between.

He's also *small* Rohan, conspicuously small for his age and, like many other small boys (Luxmoore 2006), given to compensating with grandiose claims, most of which I don't believe. He has a girlfriend with whom he claims to be having sex. At weekends, he wins fights against impossible odds, escapes from the police, catches huge fish in the local river, tries new drugs, gets impossibly drunk and has sex with older girls. He enjoys telling me all this but I never entirely believe him, hearing whatever he's saying as an exaggeration to hide the fact of his smallness, of the impotence he probably experienced as a three-year-old, aware that his father was hitting his mother and that he could do nothing about it. He enjoys being measured by me, standing upright in his socks against the wall of the counselling room as I balance a book on his head and make a mark on the wall. Stepping from beneath the book, he's keen to see whether or not he's grown. I congratulate him on every millimetre, just as I might congratulate another boy on his new hairstyle, aware how much these things matter to young people and how important it can be to have them recognized by a benignly approving parent-figure.

Sometimes we stop talking and play together, the tone of our sessions lightened, with me as a 'developmental object' (Hurry 1998), helping Rohan integrate his experienced sullen-teenager-self and his innocent playful-child-self. (His weekend stories are always about some kind of playing.) Sometimes we play conversationally, joking about football teams or TV programmes or the mistakes people make, and sometimes we play formal games of draughts, Pass-the-Pigs or Chinese chequers. Never before have we played with a pea-shooter made from an empty biro.

Davies (1998) writes that the therapist 'who sees resolution of the Oedipal in the staunch unavailability and impenetrability of her stance maintains the patient's idealization, thereby locking her into, rather than freeing her from, the constraints of incestuous desire' (p.758). In other words, a coldly opaque therapist, giving nothing away, might be aiming to teach that Oedipal satisfaction is forbidden and must be accepted as such, but, in fact, teaches that satisfaction is merely out of reach, requiring the client to work even harder to break down the therapist's tantalizingly chilly façade. For this reason, I play with Rohan. I could remain sternly distant, a father-figure with no interest in fighting with him, in winning or losing. But if I behaved in that way, I think Rohan would have left by now, consciously because of my personal 'weirdness' and unconsciously because he'd have no means of addressing his Oedipal relationship with his father. If a son unconsciously wants to get rid of his father in order to claim his mother for himself, then his first thought is to fight that father. If that father also beats up his mother, his prize, then the son's fury is redoubled. Symbolically, Rohan won his mother without a fight, his father simply having left. Now he lives with her *without* having ever triumphed over his father, enduring the intimacies of being a thirteen-year-old son living with a 33-year-old mother.

Rohan re-arms his biro with another blob of paper. He turns in his chair, grinning, and aims at my face.

I'm thrown into confusion. What's the meaning of this? Am I simply a playfellow, someone to muck around with? An older brother-figure perhaps? Or am I the Oedipal father-figure to attack? With no father in his life, should I allow the attack and not retaliate, offering him an experience of his hostility being contained? Or am I the mother he loves but also hates because he needs her so powerfully? I'm reluctant to insist that his puts the biro-weapon down ('God, it's only a biro!' he'll say) because that would be to change the rules when our previous playing has often involved us being competitive with each other, playfully hostile. I smile anxiously. This feels more personal than our previous playing and suddenly the rules aren't clear. Is Rohan allowed to shoot me in the face?

Perhaps sensing my anxiety, he shifts his aim and shoots at the wall behind me. I laugh, relieved but also vaguely disappointed. Have I spoilt his fun? Or are we learning something important about not invading each other's space?

He looks disappointed as well.

'Okay,' I say, 'you can shoot me once but I'm keeping my glasses on!'

Immediately he shoots and hits me squarely on the lens of my glasses. We both laugh.

Now he can't stop himself. He shoots at my hair, missing twice before hitting. He pretends to shoot at my face again and, when I flinch, laughs with delight.

I'm caught between one voice saying that this is harmless, Winnicottian fun and another saying that, symbolically, this is an Oedipal attack and that my response is crucial: I can't just be the meekly passive recipient of the attack or I risk shaming Rohan's masculinity by implying that his attack isn't even worthy of a response. But nor can I retaliate and risk overpowering him. Developmentally, he needs to test his power and somehow that power needs to be acknowledged.

Uselessly, I compliment him on his accuracy and remind him not to get the pea-shooter out during lessons or he'll get himself into trouble.

At this point, the school bell goes. We quickly arrange another time to meet and he dashes off, calling goodbye over his shoulder.

I'm left with an uncomfortable feeling, as if something important happened and I missed an opportunity. My discomfort increases as I scribble my notes. Somehow I feel soiled and find myself wondering whether – symbolically – Rohan has just ejaculated over me, showing me (his transferential mother) just what he can do, what's inside him.

Then I start wondering whether the bad feeling could in fact be Rohan's, whether he was showing me what he'd like to do to his father while at the same time shooting his feelings of uselessness and impotence into me. It's certainly true that I've been left feeling useless and impotent: a hapless counsellor who didn't know what to do for the best.

What has any of this got to do with sexuality? I think that Rohan was trying to make contact with me – physically and, by implication, emotionally – but the only way he knew and the only permissible way for him to do this as a frightened boy was through something disguised to look hostile. And something that *was*, in part, hostile: a hug disguised as an attack, a mischievousness mixing affection and impudence because Rohan's love and hostility towards me were bound together in an anxious, defensive muddle.

I worry that my ambivalence about receiving his gesture (worrying about the hostility rather than appreciating the love) meant that his reaching out to me was effectively spurned. Perhaps I should have welcomed his gesture, relishing rather than repudiating it, admiring the potency of his weapon.

I think back. My difficulty had always been in helping him to think about his father as a more interesting person than just 'that violent bastard' because, at the moment, half of Rohan is simply 'Bad Rohan'. Once upon a time that same violent bastard might have been loved by Rohan's mother. Out of their relationship, thirteen years ago, came Rohan. As his therapist, my intention has always been to help Rohan develop a more nuanced story because, in the beginning, his story was very simple and very brief: 'I'll kill the bastard if I ever meet him!'

I wonder whether our pea-shooter experience was Rohan's oblique way of trying to talk about his father. I wonder whether he was enacting an identification with his father (attacking me with a weapon), giving me rather than himself the problem of how to react: whether to fight off my attacker ('I'll kill the bastard!'), whether to permit the attack, putting up no resistance (did his mother do that?), or whether to negotiate with my attacker (did she do that?). In the counselling room, Rohan's and his mother's dilemmas suddenly became my dilemmas.

I also wonder about his early assertion that he was having sex with his girlfriend. He may never have had a girlfriend or have had sex with her. But perhaps his behaviour with the pea-shooter was all about having sex, about what it would be like to be alone in a room with someone, what it would be like to get out his pea-shooter and fire. In love or in hate? With permission or without? And would his pea-shooter be adequate to the task? Would the other person in the room like it or tell him to put it away and stop being so silly?

The playing between a counsellor and young person – as between a parent and child – is always a kind of expressed sexuality: agreeing and breaking rules, developing or not developing spontaneity, getting stuck and not knowing how to move on, feeling despondent or feeling delighted. Young people abandon or persist with counselling relationships in the same ways that they abandon or persist with boyfriends and girlfriends.

Whenever I lose young people, whenever they leave counselling prematurely and don't come back, it's almost always because I've failed to work with the sexuality of the relationship. I've been aware of my fondness or disregard for the young person. I've felt his or her awkwardness towards me and I've chosen to do nothing about it, concentrating instead on the overt content of our conversation: mothers, fathers, siblings, losses, disappointments…the daily stuff of therapeutic conversation.

I don't lose Rohan. He comes back the following week and immediately mentions the pea-shooter, as if he's aware that it meant something.

I ask what he's been thinking about it.

'Nothing!' he grins. 'It was just funny!' Then, making no overt connection, he talks about his father, something he's never before done without prompting. He tells me that his father met his mother when they were working together at a music festival.

I ask what else he knows about his father.

But it's as if he doesn't hear my question, beginning a long anecdote about the unfairness of schoolwork. 'I really hate the teachers! I tell all the teachers to fuck off! Most of them are scared of me. They know they can't make me do anything…'

Once again, we're back to grandiosity, except that Rohan's grandiosity always seems to be an oblique response to his father, a response to the shame of being a small boy unable to kill off the father in his head. It's always worth thinking of young people's aggression (and their stories about aggression) as defensive. It's as if the mere mention of his father frightens Rohan and has him reaching for his aggression as a way of staying safe. In our meetings, he regularly changes the subject to protect himself. I ask one question and get the answer to a completely different question…

'How's your mum, Rohan?'

'I nearly got arrested at the weekend!'

Rohan's answers usually have some defensive meaning for me to try and unpick. I think his disjointed narrative also says something about his disjointed experience of attachment. The more he's able to attach to me, the more coherent and reflective his stories become (Holmes 2001). But it's slow work. Fonagy and Allison (2014) describe 'epistemic trust' as 'an individual's willingness to consider new knowledge from another person as trustworthy, generalizable, and relevant to the self' (p.4), whereas 'epistemic vigilance' is 'the self-protective suspicion towards information coming from others that may be potentially damaging, deceptive, or inaccurate' (pp.5–6). What they mean is that our ability to learn from another person depends on the security of our attachment to that person. I would argue that attachment always has a sexual component. I think the reason why I didn't lose Rohan was because he knew that I liked him and enjoyed his company. In a sense, we were at ease with each other 'sexually' and therefore our relationship was able to withstand a pea-shooter assassination attempt!

I may not have lost Rohan but I did lose Rachel. She was fifteen and anxious to please me, chattering away about her family, friends and sexual experiences out of school. Some of these stories sounded exaggerated, made up even. I imagined that the more lurid ones were for my benefit, to keep me interested and establish her in my eyes as a grown-up, perhaps because she was scared of appearing uninteresting or childlike.

Her animated, enthusiastic conversation was at odds with her professed feeling of being 'depressed'. She would begin sessions by saying that this week, like last week, she felt 'shit', before starting to tell me exotic tales with a broad grin across her face. I'd ask questions about the more mundane parts of the stories, especially about how she was feeling at particular moments, in an attempt to demonstrate that my interest was in Rachel without exotic make-up. Yet still the tales continued.

After several sessions, I suggested to her that she sometimes sounded inauthentic, as if she didn't really mean it, as if she was telling me these stories to keep me interested.

Her expression changed. She was aghast. 'You don't get it! You just don't get it!'

I asked what it was that I didn't get. I said that I was trying hard to get it, that this was the whole point. 'What is it that I don't get? Tell me, Rachel...'

She couldn't, or wouldn't, standing up, furious. 'I've been coming here all this time,' she glared, 'and you haven't understood anything! You think I've been making it up! Is that what you think?' She was tearful now and yet *still* I found myself wondering about the authenticity of her tears.

I said that I understood her as someone trying hard to make sense of her life; as someone dealing with good and bad things, the hurts and sadnesses of her life; as someone working out who she was and who she wanted to be. But she was either too badly hurt by what I'd said or too afraid of backing down from her show of anger. (Even now, I wasn't sure how authentic that anger was.)

She walked to the door. 'Fuck you, Nick!'

I called out, trying to persuade her to come back, but she was gone.

Sometimes I say entirely the wrong thing and the young person forgives me. Sometimes I misunderstand or am unbelievably slow on the uptake and yet the young person comes back the following week. But when a young person is shamed or when there's some lingering embarrassment between us, I can lose the relationship. Publicly, young people will say that there was nothing left to talk about, or that the time of the week was inconvenient, or that things are now much better. They won't say what Rachel was probably feeling, 'You matter a lot to me, Nick. I don't know why you do and I don't like knowing that you do. I want to please you but that makes me feel uncomfortable. I can't talk to you about it and you're either not aware of it or don't want to be aware of it. Clearly you can't help me and I can't help myself. So I'm not coming back.' Murdin (2000) writes that 'Almost any unacceptable feelings of murderousness or sexuality may arouse such shame and guilt that the patient chooses to leave rather than risk revealing them...' To these unacceptable feelings, I would add the shameful feeling of *need*. Murdin goes on, 'Therapists can do no more than try to guess when there are such feelings and make them available to thought and words' (p.68).

I was left thinking... Perhaps Rachel had been sexually abused? The thought had occurred to me during our meetings and I'd explicitly asked, if only to rule out the possibility. But she'd said no, she hadn't been, scornfully screwing up her face as if it was stupid of me even to mention such a thing. But I wondered nevertheless. I wondered if she'd been trying to please me as a transferential father-lover? Perhaps she couldn't talk about her internal world, so tried to compensate with a myriad of stories about her external world? Perhaps she externalized her feelings because she had no subjective sense of herself, so could describe herself only as *doing*, never feeling? Mann (1995) observes that, however bizarre a client's behaviour may appear to be, 'rather than just seeking to sabotage the therapeutic relationship, the client is often trying to make the therapy work' (p.556). Perhaps Rachel was actually trying her best to make it work between us? Perhaps there was some truth in my comment about authenticity but, as a comment, it was disastrously timed, piercing her and leaving her exposed, so that, wounded, she lashed out as if saying, 'You don't want me! You've never wanted any of the gifts I've brought you, any of the stories I've told you! You've never understood!' It may sound overly psychoanalytical, but I wondered whether 'Fuck you, Nick!' might have translated as 'I've wanted to fuck you, Nick, to be close to you, to be special to you, but you've repudiated me. In effect, you've fucked *me*, penetrating me with your comment about inauthenticity, leaving me exposed and helpless!'

Perhaps I was the father Rachel could never have, driven only further away by her best efforts to please and entertain me. If I'd realized this earlier, perhaps we could have thought more about her father, about her longing for him and the painful distance between the two of them. Instead, I'd acted into her transference and become another rejecting father, feeling rejected by Rachel myself because she couldn't trust me enough to be 'authentic'. Perhaps because my best therapeutic efforts seemed to no avail, I felt powerless and lashed out at her? Suggesting to any young person that she sounds 'inauthentic' is a bit like accusing her of being defended, as if being defended was somehow her fault rather than an inevitable part of being human. I could simply have said that I was interested in her daily life, her daily relationships, and that I'd like to hear more about these things, not *instead* of her exotic tales but *as well as*. I could have paid much more attention to her actual father ('What would he say, Rachel? What would he think? How would he react?') rather than allowing myself to become a version of him. In short, I could have encouraged her to think about him rather than re-enact her painful relationship with him.

She never came back.

I wondered about my own sexual feelings towards Rachel. How much was I attracted or not attracted to her? Was my comment about inauthenticity a way of punishing her because I couldn't feel close to her? Was I punishing her because our conversation somehow made me feel therapeutically impotent? Was I the one being inauthentic? Nitsun (2006) disagrees with Bion's (1970) idea that a therapist should 'suspend memory and desire' in order to be fully available to the other person. 'The therapist is an embodied, gendered, sexed being and to pretend otherwise is folly,' he argues. 'The therapist must be prepared to take their position as both the object and the subject of desire' (p.250). With Rachel, I couldn't or wouldn't take that position and, as a result, I failed her.

Counsellors can't help having their own attachment histories, their own sexual histories. They try their best to be aware of these things, talking about them a lot in their own therapies so that they don't interfere in relationships with young people, but they're always there. A counsellor brings her unconscious into the room with her just as much as a young person does. She may be in the role of thoughtful, attentive, compassionate counsellor but she's also a human being and the two things can't be kept separate. Nor should she keep them separate, because, once the therapy's over, it'll be the quality of her human interactions that'll have helped (or not helped) the young person. It won't be her skilfully deployed interpretations or her ability to work with transference and counter-transference.

For some young people, counselling is effectively a first experience of safe intimacy with another person, a potentially formative experience from which other intimate relationships might follow, including sexual ones. Occasionally, a boy comes to see me, worried about his inability to have intimate relationships *not* exclusively revolving around sex. He's bored of sex, he says. He wants something more but he's not sure what. He can't name it. For him, the intimacy of a counselling relationship potentially becomes a first experience of intimacy without sex. Some boys enjoy this, relaxing, surprised at my attention and interest in their experience of the world. The intimacy of being alone in a room with another person and talking about personal things without physical touch is liberating for them.

Others can't bear it. 'What's the point?' asks sixteen-year-old Blake, full of animosity. 'You're not helping me! All we do is talk!'

'Because talking's important,' I say. 'Talking is what people always end up doing because, underneath everything, we're interested in being loved. Our big houses, our money, our flash cars... They never matter as much as being loved. Loved for who we are, rather than just loved for our bodies.'

He's taken aback. 'I don't care if people love me or not!' he says. 'Makes no difference to me!'

I've mistimed my observation. He's not ready for this and there's no point challenging his defence ('I'm sure you want to be loved really, Blake!') because he'll only cling to it more tightly ('I don't care what people think about me!'). For him to admit to a need for love would be to imply that he's come to see me for love, that he has friends for love, and that the real reason why he hates people is because he feels unloved by them. All this would be deeply embarrassing for a sixteen-year-old boy-warrior to admit.

'If I want to be loved I'll go and fuck some girl,' he says, smirking anxiously. 'I only came here to get advice about what to do!'

Developmentally, most boys separate from their mothers prematurely (Sayers 1998), identifying more readily with their fathers (Chodorow 1978) and encouraged in this by a culture that rewards them for being brave and independent while despising them for being clingy and fond. Boys find themselves out there on their own, exposed, expected to need no one, yet secretly longing to be reconnected to that original maternal love. Some boys turn their longing into hostility (an inverted form of attachment), going out with girls in order to have sex with them and then moving on ruthlessly after a few selfish encounters. This way, they can feel briefly connected without experiencing the apparent humiliation of dependency. Homosexual boys are often despised by heterosexual boys for allegedly being soft and motherly, for getting the love no longer available to the heterosexual warriors. Lesbian girls are despised for not needing the warriors' attentions in the first place.

One of the tensions in work with young people is the expectation that because they're *young*, change can be quick: six sessions and then back to the fray, at peace with the world and exuding bonhomie. Most young people certainly feel better for having told their story and that story can certainly be told in six sessions. But real therapeutic change is subtler, and the mechanism by which it happens is to be found in the relationship between the young person and the counsellor.

That relationship is always informed by the young person's sense of the counsellor as a parent-figure. Although

I'm a man, I suspect that for Blake I'm a mother-figure, expecting him to talk about feelings, doubts, misgivings and all sorts of other 'feminine' concerns. He's suspicious of me, therefore, probably desiring and despising his mother. We'll need to talk about her. Chodorow (1989) argues that:

> when a boy's mother has treated him as an extension of herself, and, at the same time, as a sexual object, he tends to continue to use his masculinity and possession of a penis as a narcissistic defence. In adulthood, he will tend to look on relationships with women for narcissistic-phallic reassurance rather than for mutual affirmation and love. (p.76)

This is precisely what Blake finds himself doing with girls.

For a boy to be emotionally reunited with his mother, able to receive her love without shame, his warrior credentials must first be acknowledged: all the ways in which he's fended for himself, dealing so bravely with the world, needing no one to help him. By extension, for boys like Blake to be emotionally intimate with a counsellor, no longer needing to recount daring feats of sexual adventure, their warrior credentials must also be acknowledged. When I sit with a boy in a counselling room and compliment him on how muscly he's becoming, he melts, suddenly prepared to talk about his feelings. When I advise him not to get into fights because he could really damage someone nowadays with his strength, he's delighted. With Blake, I have to respect his warrior defences, never pushing them aside but always appreciating how useful they've been for him, keeping him safe.

'You've done well, Blake, surviving on your own since your dad left, and no one will ever be able to take that away from you. I think that, like a lot of strong men, you've reached a point where you're strong enough to ask for some help and honest enough to know that you want more from life. Not just popularity and sex but people who'll appreciate that there's more to you than just your fearlessness...'

He looks pleased.

'People who'll appreciate that you're also a loyal person who feels things that other people don't know about. They might think they know about you, but my guess is that they don't. And trusting people to know things about you is bound to be hard after all that's happened.'

He nods in agreement and we've made a start; we've found a way of acknowledging his need without embarrassing or humiliating him.

It's exhausting to be stuck with a role, stuck with a narrow repertoire of behaviours and unable to break free. Sometimes I think that my experience as a counsellor, accepting and admiring young people for who they are, is not unlike that of the paramour or mother of some mediaeval knight, welcoming the sweaty warrior home, marvelling at his stories of triumphs in far-off lands before suggesting to him that he must be tired after so much bravery; that he might like to rest now and sleep a while, allowing his furrowed brow to be soothed. 'Like a baby,' I might think, but never say.

9

GETTING STUCK IN A ROLE

OTTO HAS HIS story and he's sticking to it. 'I'm angry all the time,' he says, as if reciting something he might have been told by a parent or teacher. 'I can't stop being angry. It's the way I am.'

And Cary has her story. 'I'm an anxious person. I get panic attacks. I've tried everything but I guess I've just got to learn to live with it. It's how I've always been.'

Young people come to counselling with an autobiographical story. Usually the story is a rigid one that needs unpicking and thinking about afresh. In it, the young person is stuck, trapped in a role from which there seems to be no escape: 'I'm angry all the time... I'm an anxious person... I'm not the kind of person boys like... Girls know I can't be trusted... I can't take anything seriously... I'm boring...'

In addition to Kohut's (1977) idea of the 'self' as a collection of internalized relationships (see Chapter 6) is the idea that we begin to develop a repertoire of roles from the beginning of our lives and that the person we become – our 'self' – is usefully thought about as a collection of roles. 'Roles do not emerge from the self, but the self may emerge from roles,' writes Moreno (1972). So a baby develops a crying role, a sucking role, a kicking role, a smiling role, a frustrated role. Through projective play, a small child might extend this basic repertoire, developing – for example – the roles of fighter, charmer, helper, spoiler, helpless slave, supreme ruler and so on. The wider the repertoire of roles we learn to play, the more resourceful and responsive we can be when situations challenge us later in life. But these roles only develop and become part of our repertoire when we attempt to play them and they're recognized and responded to by another person. We need that person as an audience, as a mirror reflecting us back to ourselves, confirming that we are indeed playing these roles in way that's recognizable and understandable to someone else playing a complementary role.

The trouble starts, and young people start coming to counselling, when they find themselves playing a narrow repertoire of roles or, like Otto and Cary, find themselves stuck in one particular role, unable to escape. So Otto is 'angry all the time' and Cary is reduced to being 'an anxious person'. Other young people might find themselves perpetually playing the role of joker or baby or cynic or flirt or group organizer or shy person or person-who-doesn't-care. Roles become entrenched from an early age because they suit us at the time or because they're the only roles that get the audience's attention or approval. If anger is the only thing that gets a response, then a baby learns to be angry. If silence always gets adult approval, then a child learns to stay silent. Sometimes we learn a role because, in the family system, it's made available to us by the unconscious workings of the family dynamic. For example, if one sibling is firmly established as The Good Child, a second sibling might find himself having to play The Bad Child or The Disappointment or The Family Problem. Roles are inter-dependent: we play them in relation to the roles being played by other people. So if a counsellor is established in the role of Having All The

Answers, a young person coming to counselling is likely to take on the role of Having No Answers.

Before we can help anyone to escape from the shackles of a stuck role, we have to understand something of how that role came into existence. Otto, it transpires, has perfectly good reasons for feeling angry. Before his parents separated, for example, his father would steal money from his mother, get drunk, and then accuse Otto's mother of stealing the money herself. His father would lock Otto's mother in the bedroom and leave her there all day until he was ready for bed, whereupon he'd lock her out of the bedroom. As a four-year-old, Otto lived through these things and more, unable to do anything.

Now he takes his revenge at the expense of a series of bemused teachers, especially men. The role of Angry Otto has become familiar: it's a safe and powerful role, but it's also a restricting role if Angry is all that his teachers ever get to know about Otto, and if Angry prevents his peers ever getting to know Otto, the potential friend, boyfriend, advisor, confidante.

As well as understanding how and why a particular role came into existence, we also have to tease out and begin to recognize the other roles that a young person might be capable of playing: the role of loving boyfriend, for example. I say to Otto that he has good reasons for being angry, that his anger makes sense. I suggest to him that he's probably also a very loyal person.

'I always stick up for my friends!'

'And when you're with them, I imagine that you're also good fun...'

He shrugs, uninterested in this, telling me instead about how he's going to beat up a boy who's been saying rude things about him.

I listen and let it go. We've established that he's not only Angry Otto but also Loyal Otto. The possibility of being Good Fun Otto is evidently too much for today. But we'll come back to the possibility of Good Fun Otto in the weeks ahead as we continue to broaden the repertoire of how he's allowed to be, at least in counselling. I'll remain interested in Angry Otto but will also be interested and keen to recognize other roles he might be capable of playing: Chatty Otto, Kind Otto, Laughing Otto, Sexual Otto, Otto-Who's-Interested-In-History, Otto-Who-Sometimes-Kisses-His-Mum-Goodnight, even though at the moment he's unconfident about being seen to play any of these roles in public. In counselling, we can begin to recognize a whole miscellany of other roles he might be capable of playing.

With sixteen-year-old Cary our work will be similar. Her anxiety is all-consuming, crippling, and yet it keeps her safe. It stops her from ever making romantic attachments and stops her taking exams because she's too anxious to go into the examination room. In that sense, Anxious Cary protects her from the possibilities of sex and academic failure, and this may have suited her in the past. The trouble is that now she finds herself struggling with the constraints of the role, wanting to break free but afraid to break free. If she weren't so stuck in the role of Anxious Cary, she might be able to be angry, sexy, funny, gregarious, challenging: she might be able to play all sorts of other, as yet undeveloped, roles. Developing any of these roles will start by having them recognized by her counsellor in the same way that a baby develops an initial role repertoire under the mirroring, recognizing gaze of a parent-figure. Counselling might be a chance to practise roles she's not yet ready to play outside the safety of the counselling room. In the room, she works hard to convince me that anxious is all she is. But whenever there are glimpses of other, fledgling roles – Cary Who Likes Singing, Cary The Bad Tempered, Cary The Good Friend, Cary The Argumentative, Cary-Who-Fancies-Certain-Members-Of-Boy-Bands – I recognize them quickly and am clearly interested in them. And whenever we've spent time talking about these things, she quickly tells me a long tale of anxiety as if to remind me that she's still officially Anxious Cary and I'm not to forget!

We develop and jettison roles as we go through life. A few we retain because they continue to protect us or are especially rewarding but, with luck, we're able to slip in and out of roles appropriately and skilfully like so many chameleons adapting to the challenges of changing circumstances. Our ability to do this depends, in part, on the extent to which the people around us are able to slip in and out of roles themselves, comfortable with their own infinite variety. I remember disclosing to a young person that I'd probably be spending New Year's Eve, not out celebrating with friends, but at home watching a box set. 'Preferably,' I added, 'something with lots of killing!'

Her eyes widened. 'You're joking, aren't you? You don't really watch stuff like that!'

I promised her that I was no different from lots of other people when it came to car chases, shoot-outs and murders.

She said nothing but I sensed her disappointment that someone she respected as a serious-minded counsellor (the role in which I'd cast myself) could be so base. It was as if I'd betrayed her by not sticking to my familiar role.

There's a time and a place for disillusioning young people, and perhaps I misjudged this. But who other people are – who they *really* are – is a preoccupation for young people fascinated by the secret lives of parents, teachers, counsellors, friends, and fascinated by the possibility of having secret lives themselves. 'What am I like *really*? What do I *really* feel? What do I *really* want?' They play with the idea that they may not be all that they seem, yet sometimes we do them no favours by suggesting that there's some quintessential self hidden away somewhere inside them. 'You're not yourself!' we say when they're unhappy or angry or behaving in unusual ways. And when they're caught up in a dilemma, we advise them, 'Be true to yourself! Listen to yourself! Do what's right for you!' We exhort them to realize their 'full potential', as if potential was predetermined and fixed rather than fluid and constantly subject to the capricious, emergent effects of experience. We talk of 'self-actualization', as if we reach a point in our lives where our 'true' selves are finally revealed.

The idea that people are complex, capable of playing many different, changing roles, and that they may not be all that they seem, provokes mixed reactions in young people. They're fascinated, for sure, but at other times they'd prefer things to remain simple with the people around them clearly and narrowly defined. They'll readily accuse each other of being 'two-faced' as if they're surprised that someone's capable of saying one thing to one person and another thing to another person. I suspect that these accusations are fuelled less by genuine surprise than by the disappointment that it's no longer possible to live in a child's world where people are simply who they're supposed to be, fitted out with 'characters' and 'personalities', deploying a limited and predictable repertoire of roles.

Different young people are ready to be disillusioned at different times and confessing to my secret enjoyment of violent box sets may have been too much for that young person at the time. But we give young people permission to enlarge the repertoire of roles they can play when we're able to acknowledge our own complexities and contradictions. The idea of an 'authentic' self waiting for a young person somewhere just out of reach isn't very helpful (as I found to my cost with Rachel in the previous chapter). Nor is it helpful to be with a counsellor who, in the interests of consistency, strives to be the same every week, never wavering in his or her demeanour in a room that also never changes from week to week. We know from neuroscience that a depressed parental face is likely to be copied and internalized by a baby (Gerhardt 2004). So when Winnicott (1971) describes the importance of a parent and child playing together, he's describing a role repertoire developing through playfulness and interaction. Moreno's (1961) description of anxiety makes sense:

> Everybody is expected to live up to his official role in life; a teacher is to act as a teacher, a pupil as a pupil, and so forth. But the individual craves to embody far more roles than those he is allowed to act out in life... Every individual is filled with different roles in which he wants to become active and that are present in him in different stages of development. It is from the active pressure which these multiple individual units exert upon the manifest official role that a feeling of anxiety is often produced. (p.63)

In order to help young people like Cary and Otto, counsellors need to avoid becoming trapped in a role themselves. Like parents and children, counsellors and young people have to learn to play together. Of course, in the early days when a young person is new to counselling and is most baby-like in the relationship, his or her counsellor will need to deploy a more limited repertoire of roles, letting the 'baby' absorb things slowly, not going too fast and not overloading the baby with too much new experience. But as the 'baby' becomes more confident, the counsellor has to respond, not only by mirroring and affirming the young person's expanding role repertoire but by initiating and modelling new role possibilities.

This begs questions for counsellors about self-disclosure. 'How much should I remain in role as the solid, reliable attachment-figure who says nothing or very little about herself? How much should my focus stay always on the young person, and where does this fit with Winnicott's ideas about learning and development through playfulness and interaction? How much do young people get stuck in counselling because, in fact, *the counsellor* gets stuck in a role from which he or she can't escape? And if I were to be more spontaneous and sometimes say a little more about myself, is this young person ready?'

I'm not arguing for counsellors to start off-loading their own pathologies onto unsuspecting young people. Absolutely not! But given what we know about mirroring and neuroscience and the brain developing through relationships with other people, I do wonder whether the old psychoanalytic assumptions about remaining opaque and disclosing nothing, assumptions adopted by many counsellors, sometimes create a stasis, an *asexual* stasis in the counselling room analogous to a baby trying to develop new roles under the gaze of a parent who remains impassive: never surprised, never delighted, never aghast, never initiating anything herself.

One day I arrive to meet with Angry Otto, only to find that our normal room has been taken by someone else.

Instead of staying tip-lipped, I curse. 'God, it's so annoying when that happens!' I say to him. 'We've been the ones using that room for weeks and now they've barged in there and don't even say sorry!'

'Doesn't really matter,' he says calmly. 'I don't mind meeting in a classroom if there's one free.'

Because roles are inter-dependent, I think that the experience of his counsellor taking on the angry role frees Otto to take on the role of Placatory Sensible Person Dealing With A Setback. I haven't seen him play this role before. Usually he's the one sitting there cursing a whole series of recent setbacks and I'm the one playing the role of Placatory Sensible Person.

With Anxious Cary I learn to remember little things like the name of her budgerigar, her favourite meal, her most hated TV character, the book she's reading, her dream holiday destination, her favourite type of chocolate. I enjoy hearing about the fortunes of her various boy bands. Our conversations about these everyday things become opportunities for us to laugh, agreeing with each other, disagreeing with each other, enthusing together and separately. In short, we start trying out new roles together.

Growing up, it's easy to get stuck as Angry Otto or Anxious Cary, as the seducer or seductress, as the academic or sporty person, as the drama queen or disruptive student, as the disengaged boy or shy girl... It's tempting to play these roles because they're familiar ('If that's what you think I'm like, then that's what I'll *be* like!') and yet it's frustrating to be typecast. Young people's attempts to try out new roles only succeed when these new roles are recognized by other people happily playing a wide variety of roles themselves. Creativity is at the heart of this process…

10

ANGER, CREATIVITY AND SEXUALITY

AS SOON AS she's old enough, Sara's going to get two tattoos: one of a tortoise and one of a butterfly. She doesn't know why exactly, 'I just like them!'

As our conversation goes on, the meaning of the tortoise and the butterfly becomes clearer. Tortoise Sara keeps her thoughts and feelings to herself, keeps her head down and stays out of the limelight. Butterfly Sara emerges occasionally but is more of an aspiration, a sense of how life *could* be: colourful and unburdened, flitting from one thing to the next. Tortoise Sara stays safe but feels ignored. Butterfly Sara gets lots of attention but that brings its own problems…

How do professionals encourage a girl like Sara to be as much of a butterfly as possible without losing her ability to retreat into a tortoise shell if and when she chooses? How do we help a tortoise who gets stuck, afraid to come out from under her shell? Or a butterfly who gets frightened, wounded by other people's suspicion and jealousy?

'I might as well give up,' says Sara. 'There's no point! People are always going to be horrible!'

She's had a bad experience at a party with one of her friends – drunk – claiming that Sara was 'up herself' and encouraging other girls to be rude about her.

'They always do it,' she goes on. 'They always say horrible things about everyone. Not just about me. You can't do anything without one of them saying something. They're always bitching about someone!'

'And they're your friends...'

'I've always gone round with them, ever since primary school. If I didn't have them, I'd have no one to go round with.'

I ask if there are other girls she'd like to get to know.

'There are, but they've already got their groups.'

She's criticized by her so-called friends for daring to be a butterfly in her choice of clothes, in her desire to talk to other people at parties, in her determination to do well at school and in her once-mentioned interest in being in a school musical. With her friends around, she's obliged to retreat into a tortoise shell but dreads being stuck there for ever.

Together, we bear her sense of the hopelessness of the situation. We try not to panic and try not to come up with cheap, unrealistic solutions. At the same time I remain determinedly interested in Sara the butterfly as she tells me about shopping for unusual clothes at weekends, about the people she meets in her dad's shop, about the novel she's reading and about auditioning (despite her friends) for the musical.

To my delight, she gets a part in the chorus. This means lots of rehearsals because members of the chorus are on and off stage throughout the production. I start hearing rehearsal stories about people in the show and how much she likes them: people she's never talked to before. Predictably, her friends are taking no interest whatsoever in any of this, but somehow Sara's undeterred.

She glows with pride when we meet the week after the show. 'It's the most fun I've ever had! It's been amazing! I've got to know so many people!' A few social invitations have already come in from people who were in the show. It's as if butterfly Sara is re-emerging, confident and colourful, and she's finding ways of dealing with her old friends, gradually seeing less and less of them. Apparently they give her 'evil' looks whenever they see her talking to someone from the show and they make disparaging remarks about actors being 'gay' and 'weird'. Our meetings become opportunities to take stock, thinking together about where her butterfly confidence comes from and what takes it away. She still has her tortoise shell available for future use (and there'll undoubtedly be times when she'll need it), but our meetings are helping to make it clear that being a butterfly is an interesting, worthwhile thing to be.

There are plenty of young people with highly developed tortoise shells. Some are shy. Some stay at home. Some only do as they're told. Some might eventually be described as 'depressed'. They're not born with tortoise shells but grow them in order to deal with the disruption and personalities around them. Some develop shells because their parents, too, have shells, and know no other way of dealing with life. Unlike Sara, many of these young people seem quite unable to uncover their butterfly potential. Indeed, some appear to have no such potential at all. As I described in the previous chapter, they're stuck in a role, seemingly unable to break free.

Winnicott (1971) describes creativity, or the lack of it, as 'a colouring of the whole attitude to external reality' (p.65).

A baby's creativity, he argues, 'is directly related to the quality and quantity of environmental provision at the beginning or in the early phases of each baby's living experience' (p.71). If our parents are scared of the world, we're likely to internalize that fear; if they respond narrowly to life, we're likely to do the same.

Like other supportive relationships, counselling provides young people with an alternative environment in which to try things out, finding small butterfly wings and flying, however briefly, without shame. Talking with a counsellor is a creative act, a creative experience that potentially colours external reality differently.

Alice and I are meeting for the first time. She says nothing as we walk to my counselling room and, once inside, once we've finished talking about confidentiality and about what to expect from counselling, she begins by telling me in the most deadpan way, 'It's my anger. I get angry a lot in school, so they said to come and see you.'

Immediately I'm encouraged. They may often express their anger inappropriately, but feeling angry in the first place means that young people are alive, refusing to be cowed. They're angry because they care (Luxmoore 2006), and Alice will almost certainly have things to be angry about, not least because she's a fourteen-year-old girl and therefore expected to be all things to all people.

She tells me more but speaks without emphasis, flatly, avoiding my eye, with no suggestion of anger in her voice, as if her life is of no interest whatsoever, as if she's bored with herself.

We spend a long time talking about her life, about living with a strict, old-fashioned grandmother who, according to Alice, doesn't understand modern teenagers, and about Alice's mother who lives miles away. (She's never met her father.) When I ask about this unusual domestic situation, Alice says that she doesn't know why she lives with her grandmother; she's never asked. But by the time we meet the following week, she's asked her grandmother and discovered that it's because her mother was ill when Alice was born. When I continue to be interested in this most important part of her story, Alice goes away, asks her grandmother again and, returning, tells me that her mother was apparently no good with kids.

Our therapeutic task will be to get Alice interested in herself and her story. But that's going to take a while if no one's been very interested in her until now, or if they've only been interested in her being seen and not heard. Anger might have become Alice's way of getting noticed, her way of saying that her life doesn't make much sense but that she's still here, still alive.

I ask about her mother: what she's like, what she does, what she says...

Alice can't think of anything to say. 'My mum's let herself go,' she announces finally. 'She wears really bad clothes and doesn't do her hair or anything. I remember one time, I was on the bus with her and it was really embarrassing because everyone was looking at us!' She goes on to complain that her grandmother doesn't understand about make-up.

I ask what she means. 'Make-up' could be a euphemism for anything.

'She's never shown me how to put it on. She doesn't *like* make-up!'

Disapproving of a girl's make-up could mean disapproving of her growing up, of her choice of friends, of the boys in her life, of the distant possibility of sex...

'I've had to learn how to do make-up myself.'

I say that her make-up looks good today.

'Do you think so?' She's obviously pleased. 'I didn't really have time to put it on, and it's school, so they don't let you wear much.'

'But you put it on anyway...'

'Yeah! I don't care! They can make me take it off but I'll still go and put it back on!'

It's as if she's beginning to be interested in herself, at least in how she presents herself: a tortoise interested, perhaps, in becoming a butterfly. The next time we meet, her hair looks different.

'I've had it cut. And they put some colour in it. But I didn't tell my Gran and I still don't think she's even noticed!'

I ask if Alice has people fancying her.

'No!'

'Really?'

'No way! I don't go round with boys if that's what you mean... There's one boy who likes me, though. Well, I think he might like me. I don't know if he does really.' She and her friend are going to meet this boy on Saturday.

The following week, I ask how that went. Nothing happened because Alice had to go shopping with her grandmother. I ask if she and the boy are planning another meeting.

They are.

If her depressed mother and old-fashioned grandmother have been particularly dull mirrors for Alice to look into, mirrors in which she saw herself as deadpan, flat and uninteresting, my role has been as an 'enlivening mirror' (Alvarez 1992), interested in her story, approving of her make-up and hair, curious about her first, tentative forays into the world of boys. Creativity and sexuality are entwined. A narrowed, uninterested, unconfident creativity will express itself as a narrowed, uninterested, unconfident sexuality. And these things will be learned from a parental environment that notices (or doesn't), that's interested (or isn't), that's encouraging (or isn't). My guess is that, without an enlivening mirror, Alice's creative expression was reduced to a howl of angry protest, lashing out at school, alerting people to the fact that something wasn't right.

Tilly's also angry, lashing out verbally. 'I hate everyone!' she says, glaring at me. 'I hate my friends! I hate my family!'

I'm taken aback, doing my best to remember that these are Tilly's defences, her ways of dealing with life and that my job is to understand how these defences came to be. She isn't a child. She's seventeen, applying for university and, when she's not busy with schoolwork, she works conscientiously with younger students in school, helping them with English and Maths. They love her.

'I hate my life! I don't care about university! I don't care about anything!'

I like her anger. I say this to her and she's surprised, unsure what to say, unsure whether she's supposed to be a serious, studious, conscientious seventeen-year-old or a raging child. It's as if a much younger Tilly got left behind somewhere down the road and is now running to catch up with her seventeen-year-old self, determined not to be forgotten.

I ask about her childhood. She's the eldest of three children. When she was five and starting school, her younger brother was dangerously ill at the same time as her mother was pregnant with Tilly's sister. It's easy to see why Tilly's anger would have needed to stay hidden with everything that was probably going on at the time. It makes sense. What matters is that Tilly can now begin to integrate her childlike anger and studious, conscientious, grown-up self. She won't endear herself to university lecturers and fellow students by shouting out that she hates them!

Young people need their anger. They need it to fuel their assertiveness, their determination, their refusal to be cowed. Perhaps, at some unconscious level, Tilly knows this and is trying to do something about it before it's too late, reclaiming the anger that got left behind when she was five.

But it's hard. She glares at me. 'I hate counselling! Listening to everyone's problems… People should just get on with their lives!'

'Like you had to?'

'See what I mean!' she says. 'You're reading stuff into everything I say. God, I hate that!'

I feel like saying 'So why have you come to see me, Tilly?' but that would be to take revenge on her for challenging me. She's come because she needs help. To admit this would be humiliating. With her secret need for help exposed, stroppy Tilly would walk out and never come back. But trying to reason with a ranting five-year-old is of limited value, and Tilly is also a seventeen-year-old capable of very sophisticated reasoning, on high intellectual alert for counsellors glibly turning attacks back on the attacker. Seventeen-year-olds expect to be treated as philosophical equals, whereas five-year-olds expect answers; they expect people to come to their rescue and make everything all right. Their anger is both an expression of frustration and a way of coercing the person on the receiving end. When the adult and child parts of a young person are split in this way, the adult part is usually ashamed of the child part. So it helps to explain to the adult part what's happening as transparently as possible, acknowledging that the adult part is doing a good job and explaining to the young person why the child part still exists.

'Your anger makes sense,' I say to her as she stares angrily at the wall. 'It sounds as if when you were young you had reason to be angry. But with all that was going on it would have felt impossible and unfair to say what you were feeling. So your anger probably never went away, Tilly. It got put in a box for later. And now that you're adult and confident and strong enough to look at it, you're opening the box. You're not mad. You're angry because you care and because – when you were young – no one listened. It doesn't mean that you're not also an extremely thoughtful person who takes responsibility and is kind to all sorts of people, a person who works hard and tries her best. You're all of these things. *And* you're angry!'

She's quiet, thinking about this as a way of understanding herself. My guess is that she'll be all right in the long run because – however childlike it may be – she has her anger and is able to express it. Other girls aren't so fortunate. Their anger gets squashed, silenced, turned into depression, held inside as something bad, shameful and impossible for a 'nice' girl to acknowledge. Their sexual expressiveness will almost certainly suffer the same fate.

Tasha's anger, for example, is almost impossible to detect. As she talks about her life, she sighs wearily, repeatedly ending her stories with 'But what can you do!' She seems to be putting on weight, comforting herself, I suspect, with food.

A few months ago, she felt that she had to make a choice. Or rather, that a choice was being made for her, that she had *no* choice. The only girl in a family of younger boys, her parents expected her to do all the chores: not only the household chores but the babysitting ones as well. She put up with this, but it became harder once she started going out with nineteen-year-old Jamie, unemployed with a criminal record and with a son he was no longer allowed to see. Tasha was trying to do justice to her boyfriend, to her work at school and to her life at home. Her parents became angrier and angrier, insisting that she stay indoors, that the family had to come first and that, unless the chores were done, there would be trouble.

'But the boys never had to do anything!' she tells me. 'It was always me! Whenever Mum and Dad knew I'd arranged to meet up with Jamie, they'd make up something else that I had to do at home so that I couldn't see him. It was embarrassing!'

Phillips (2005) writes: 'Whether one wants to be one of the nice and good, or whether one wants to feel rather more excitedly alive is an acute dilemma for most adolescents' (p.149). For many, he argues, 'Sexual desire is the route out of the family' (p.127). I agree with him. With all those hormones brewing and bubbling and refusing to be ignored, sex becomes an impulsive expression of creativity for some young people, one that can't help but involve meeting new people, taking new risks, enjoying new sensations and satisfactions. For some young people, sex and the pursuit of sex become ways of being alive, no longer stuck at home, no longer 'depressed' but living creatively, the erotic instinct fighting the death instinct (Freud 1920).

Her father eventually gave Tasha an ultimatum: Do as you're told or leave home. A row followed and she was obliged to leave, moving in with Jamie, sharing his bedroom in a rented two-bedroom house where, again, she found herself expected to do the chores for her boyfriend and his father.

I ask what she feels like saying to them.

'Dunno,' she says, avoiding the question. 'Sometimes it's all right, though, and sometimes Jamie actually says thanks if I've cleaned the house or something.'

'And that's enough?'

'Well, sort of. There's nothing else he can say really, is there?'

'He could help you with the cleaning!'

'He'd never do that,' she says, smiling at the very thought.

'Because?'

'He just wouldn't.'

'Because he doesn't think it's his job?'

'Probably.'

Tasha is like other girls who have learned to please people (especially men), keeping them happy by never complaining and never getting angry. For some of these girls, a future of domestic servitude and clinical depression awaits. Tasha and I could be angry together, but the trouble is that anger isn't the only thing she feels. She believes that she loves Jamie and that she's lucky to have him as her boyfriend. So my job isn't to cast aspersions or tell her that she'd be better off on her own, much as I might think that. At the moment, she has nowhere else to go and no one else to take an interest in her. Jamie is untouchable.

'I wonder whether – as well as loving Jamie and enjoying being with him and all the good things you have together – I wonder whether there might be a part of you, Tasha – even if it's a small part – that might feel pissed off with him and with his dad?'

'I do get pissed off sometimes,' she says, 'when they expect me to do everything round the house.'

'The same as at home?'

'Yeah, just like at home.'

'And at those times, what do you feel like saying?'

'Dunno really…'

'When you're on your own and they can't hear, I wonder what you're saying to them in your head?'

'Nothing really…' She can't do it.

I try again. 'I imagine you sitting them down, Tasha, tying them to their chairs, gagging them…'

She smiles at the thought.

'…and saying something like, "Jamie I mainly love you and I'm glad we're together but sometimes it feels as if you and your dad expect me to do everything round the house and that feels unfair…"'

She nods.

'"…and at those times I feel unhappy and pissed off."'

She looks blank.

I ask her if I've understood correctly.

She nods.

'So what would you say to them? In *your* words?'

'That I don't like it?'

I prompt her. 'That it's annoying?'

'Yeah.'

'Annoying and… And what?'

'Annoying and unfair?'

It's my turn to nod. 'I think it *is* unfair, Tasha. And I'm not surprised that you feel annoyed. I think you've got a right to feel annoyed.'

She looks surprised. And pleased.

We're giving her back her anger, affirming it, exploring it, practising it in our conversations, and slowly – very slowly – becoming more confident with it as a vital, creative part of who she's allowed to be: a girl who loves people, who tries her best. And who feels angry as an essential part of being alive.

Storr (1972) describes creativity as both the expression and attempted resolution of internal or unconscious conflict. If a young person caught between love and hate, between duty and desire, between childhood and adulthood can find some creative expression, then these conflicts feel less onerous, less stuck. There are psychotherapeutic methods based on this idea, methods that work through the medium of creative arts, using music, drama, painting, sculpture and dance, for example. There are other methods that use horticulture and animals – growing plants, caring for animals – as creative opportunities intended to resolve something inside us: making us feel more useful, more peaceful, less trapped. And, by the same token, there are hundreds of young people for whom everyday activities such as playing sport, looking after children or simply making friends represent creative opportunities. There are young people who write poems and songs, who design computer games. But for most young people, the simple fact of talking to someone is creative: taking the risk of confiding in another person, negotiating power, bearing the uncertainty of the relationship without panicking.

Rhianna comes to see me because she can't stop feeling anxious, especially about the approaching mock exams. 'If I can't manage them,' she says, 'then how am I going to manage when it comes to the real ones?' By her own admission, she's good at schoolwork, a lot is expected of her and she worries about this. But at the same time, she's a very friendly person, smiling brightly as she tells me about these things. She sounds so sensible that I find it hard to imagine her ever messing up her exams. And yet she says that she once had a panic attack in an exam.

I tell her that, in my experience, 'anxiety' is a word we use to describe some sort of conflict inside ourselves. That conflict might, I say, be the conflict between wanting to succeed yet being afraid of failing. She nods, understanding immediately. I wonder about other conflicts in her life… We talk about her family but, by the sound of it, there's no tyrannical father urging her on, no ambitious mother expecting her daughter to live out her own unlived life. Her parents put no pressure on her, she says. In fact, they keep telling her to relax. But she's the eldest and feels responsible. She feels that she has to do well.

I ask what makes her angry.

'There isn't anything really,' she says, smiling, 'apart from my brother. He can be annoying sometimes.' Her friends are okay, she says. She helps them with their love lives, listening to their woes, giving them advice.

I ask if they listen to her.

'Not really,' she says, 'but I don't mind because I like helping them.'

'What about when you're feeling angry or sad, Rhianna? Or when you're feeling anxious? Do they listen then?'

She shakes her head. 'I don't really get like that when I'm with them,' she says, smiling.

I'm unconvinced, partly because I think that all healthy people get angry sometimes (Luxmoore 2006), and partly because my guess is that her anger may well be the cause of the so-called 'anxiety': anger that gets trapped, repressed, disavowed, anger waging a silent war against responsible, sensible, smiling Rhianna.

When I ask whether she has people flirting with her the way they flirt with her friends, she looks forlorn. 'Not really.'

'Would you like to have people flirting with you?'

'I don't know,' she says. 'Maybe. In a way. But I'm not really bothered.'

The last thing I want to suggest to her is that she *ought* to be bothered. She can take these things at her own pace and is perfectly entitled to avoid romantic relationships with boys or girls for as long as she wants. It's just that she looked forlorn when I asked and seemed vaguely resentful about spending so much of her time supporting other people through their various entanglements. My guess is that her anxiety *is* related to her anger, to the conflict between Responsible Rhianna (the role she's learned to play) and Angry Rhianna (the role she hasn't). My guess is that, without her anger, she'll never be available to go out with a boy or girl because her sexual expressiveness will be blunted, held back by an inability to be angry. So she can smile her responsible, sensible, kind smile but can't smile a wicked, flirtatious, dangerous smile. A girl confident with anger might feel more confident about flirting with someone, knowing that she can retreat from the situation at any moment, that her anger will keep her safe. A girl confident with anger will be more likely to have likes and dislikes; whereas Rhianna, I suspect, will be trying to see the good in everyone. I want to help her discover her anger because I think she'll feel less anxious, less conflicted if she can be Angry Rhianna *as well as* Responsible Rhianna and see no contradiction.

I ask whether she sometimes – just occasionally – feels like telling the whole world to fuck off.

Hearing me swear, she looks taken aback, then relaxes and nods her head. 'Sometimes…'

'Like when…?'

'What do you mean?'

'Like when people are annoying you? Or when they don't listen? Or when your brother's pissing you off…?'

She talks about her brother, about the annoying things he does and gets away with, about her parents' indulgence of him, about the things she never got away with when she was that age. I begin to hear the anger, still polite, but anger nonetheless. I explain that I like angry people because they're passionate, because they believe in fairness, because they care a lot. I tell her that I like the fact that she works hard at school *and* feels angry about things, that she supports her friends *and* feels angry when they don't listen.

She looks confused.

When we meet again, two weeks later, I say I like the way she's coloured the ends of her hair. She says nothing. I ask how things have been and ask especially about what's been pissing her off. I choose 'pissing off' carefully, partly to give Sensible Rhianna permission to swear a little and partly to widen our shared vocabulary. She doesn't have to use these words, but implicitly has permission to do so if she chooses, if she wants to experiment.

And she does start to use these words from time to time, seemingly more comfortable in acknowledging her likes and dislikes, her pleasures and displeasures. We talk a lot about having mixed feelings: wanting to do well in her exams and sometimes feeling like giving up; wanting to support her friends and yet sometimes wanting to tell them to piss off;

loving people and sometimes loathing them. She reports that she's been feeling a bit less anxious. The mock exams were fine.

I don't ask more about flirting with other people. That can come later. For now, talking itself is enough.

ENDPIECE

ANOTHER DAY AT work, another bunch of young people to see. Including Paul.

We've been meeting every fortnight for the last two years, thinking about his terrible exam results, his intermittent attempts to work harder, his abiding lack of confidence, his attempts to dress fashionably on a tiny budget, to act cool, to style his hair differently, to talk the talk.

We've discussed the way he might come across to other people. Paul was bullied when he was younger and has never regained whatever confidence he might once have had. Then his parents split up. Then his mother's interest turned to her new boyfriend. Then his only friend started hanging out with other people. It goes on... He's eighteen now, still without friends he can rely on, still perceived as a geek, still trying too hard in some situations, I suspect, and not trying hard enough in others. He wants to do well but is easily discouraged, scared of the future and lonely, afraid that no one will ever love him, that he'll die a failure, the only person in the history of the world (as he sees it) never to have had sex, never even to have kissed someone, other than perhaps some drunken person giving out birthday kisses. In our sessions, he's ranted, been stuck, cried and regularly felt like giving up.

Today he comes into my room in a hurry. Something's up, I think to myself, or else he's escaping from other boys in the corridor. He sits down. Unusually, he doesn't want a hot drink. My heart sinks.

And then he smiles. 'I've met someone…'

I try not to get my hopes up. 'You have?'

'You know the party I was telling you about… Well, I actually went to it. I didn't really want to, but I did. And it turned out I was right and I only knew a couple of people. But I sort of got talking to this person…' His face is alight. 'Well, I know this is going to be hard to believe, but she actually seemed to quite like me! And we spent the whole party together, just talking! Turned out she likes some of the same things I do and we even have the same taste in music, weirdly. And I don't know… We just got on!'

I say how pleased I am. 'Will you see her again?'

He can barely contain himself. 'Well, that's the bit I haven't told you… After the party, we went back to her house!'

I can feel my eyes widening.

'And… You know!'

'What do I know?'

He's about to burst. 'It happened!'

'It happened?'

'It happened!'

'And… It was good?'

He shakes his head. 'No, it wasn't good… It was fucking wonderful!'

I feel like crying.

REFERENCES

Alvarez, A. (1992) *Live Company: Psychoanalytic Psychotherapy with Autistic, Borderline, Deprived and Abused Children.* London and New York: Tavistock/Routledge.

Alvarez, A. (2012) *The Thinking Heart: Three Levels of Psychoanalytic Therapy with Disturbed Children.* Hove: Routledge.

Balint, M. (1935) 'Critical Notes on the Theory of the Pregenital Organizations of the Libido.' In *Primary Love and Psychoanalytic Technique.* New York: Liveright.

Baron-Cohen, S. (2004) *The Essential Difference.* London: Penguin Books.

Barter, C., McCarry, M., Berridge, D. and Evans, K. (2009) *Partner Exploitation and Violence in Teenage Intimate Relationships.* London: NSPCC.

Bettelheim, B. (1976) *The Uses of Enchantment.* London: Thames and Hudson.

Bion, W.R. (1970) *Attention and Interpretation.* London: Tavistock Publications.

Bramley, W. (2014, December) 'Serious play and playful seriousness: implications for psychotherapy.' *Bulletin 60. The Oxford Psychotherapy Society.*

Briggs, S. (2008) *Working with Adolescents and Young Adults.* Basingstoke: Palgrave Macmillan.

Butler, J. (1990) *Gender Trouble.* Abingdon: Routledge.

Chodorow, N.J. (1978) *The Reproduction of Mothering: Psychoanalysis and the Sociology of Gender.* Berkeley, CA: University of California Press.

Chodorow, N.J. (1989) *Feminism and Psychoanalytic Theory.* New Haven, CT, and London: Yale University Press.

Chodorow, N.J. (1994) *Femininities, Masculinities, Sexualities.* London: Free Association Books.

Cohen, J. (2013) *The Private Life.* London: Granta Publications.

Coy, M., Kelly, L., Elvines, F., Garner, M. and Kanyeredzi, A. (2013) *'Sex without consent, I suppose that is rape': How Young People in England Understand Sexual Consent.* London: Office of the Children's Commissioner.

Davies, J.M. (1998) 'Between the disclosure and foreclosure of erotic transference-countertransference can psychoanalysis find a place for adult sexuality?' *Psychoanalytic Dialogues, The International Journal of Relational Perspectives 8*, 6, 747–766. doi:10.1080/10481889809539292

De Beauvoir, S. (1949) *The Second Sex*. London: Penguin Books.

Diamond, N. (2014) 'On Bowlby's Legacy: Further Explorations.' in M. Marrone (ed.) *Attachment and Interaction*. London: Jessica Kingsley Publishers.

Ensler, E. (2001) *The Vagina Monologues*. London: Virago.

Fonagy, P. (2001) *Attachment Theory and Psychoanalysis*. New York: Other Press.

Fonagy, P. and Allison, E. (2014) 'The role of mentalising and epistemic trust in the therapeutic relationship.' *Psychotherapy 51*, 3, 372–380. doi:10.1037/a0036505.

Foucault, M. (1990, 1992) *The History of Sexuality (Vols. 1–3)*. London: Penguin Books.

Freud, S. (1905) 'Three Essays on the Theory of Sexuality.' In *The Standard Edition of the Complete Psychological Works of Sigmund Freud (Vol. 7)*. London: Hogarth Press.

Freud, S. (1908) 'Civilised Sexual Morality and Modern Nervous Illness.' In *The Standard Edition of the Complete Psychological Works of Sigmund Freud (Vol. 9)*. London: Hogarth Press.

Freud, S. (1912) 'On the Universal Tendency to Debasement in the Sphere of Love.' In *The Standard Edition of the Complete Psychological Works of Sigmund Freud (Vol. 11)*. London: Hogarth Press.

Freud, S. (1914) 'Some Reflections on Schoolboy Psychology.' In *The Standard Edition of the Complete Psychological Works of Sigmund Freud (Vol. 13)*. London: Hogarth Press.

Freud, S. (1915) 'Observations on Transference Love.' In *The Standard Edition of the Complete Psychological Works of Sigmund Freud (Vol. 12)*. London: Hogarth Press.

Freud, S. (1920) 'Beyond the Pleasure Principle.' In *The Standard Edition of the Complete Psychological Works of Sigmund Freud (Vol. 18)*. London: Hogarth Press.

Freud, S. (1923) 'The Ego and the Id.' In *The Standard Edition of the Complete Psychological Works of Sigmund Freud (Vol. 19)*. London: Hogarth Press.

Frosh, S. (1999) *The Politics of Psychoanalysis*. New York: New York Universities Press.

Gabbard, G.O. and Twernlow, S.W. (1989) 'The Lovesick Therapist.' in G.O. Gabbard (ed.) *Sexual Exploitation in Professional Relationships*. Washington, DC: American Psychiatric Press.

Gerhardt, S. (2004) *Why Love Matters: How Affection Shapes a Baby's Brain*. Hove: Brunner-Routledge.

Gilligan, J. (2000) *Violence: Reflections on Our Deadliest Epidemic*. London: Jessica Kingsley Publishers.

Glasser, M. (1979) 'Some Aspects of the Role of Aggression in the Perversions.' In L. Rosen (ed.) *Sexual Deviation*. Oxford, New York, NY, and Toronto: Oxford University Press.

Gomez, L. (1997) *An Introduction to Object Relations*. London: Free Association Books.

Graham, P. (2004) *The End of Adolescence*. Oxford: Oxford University Press.

Hartley, L.P. (1997) *The Go-Between*. London: Penguin Books. (Original work published 1953)

Hiller, J. (2006) 'Sex, Mind and Emotion Through the Life Course: A Biopsychosocial Perspective.' In J. Hiller, H. Wood and W. Bolton (eds.) *Sex, Mind, and Emotion*. London: Karnac Books.

Hines, M. (2004) *Brain Gender*. Oxford: Oxford University Press.

Hines, S. (2007) *Transforming Gender*. Bristol: The Policy Press.

Hobson, R.F. (1985) *Forms of Feeling: The Heart of Psychotherapy*. London: Routledge.

Holmes, J. (2001) *The Search for the Secure Base*. Hove: Routledge.

Holmes, J. (2010) *Exploring in Security: Towards an Attachment-informed Psychoanalytic Psychotherapy*. Hove: Routledge.

Horne, A. (2012) 'Body and Soul: Developmental Urgency and Impasse.' In A. Horne and M. Lanyado (eds.) *Winnicott's Children*. Hove: Routledge.

Hurry, A. (1998) 'Psychoanalysis and Developmental Theory.' In A. Hurry (ed.) *Psychoanalysis and Developmental Theory*. London: Karnac Books.

Jensen, F.E. and Ellis Nutt, A. (2015) *The Teenage Brain*. London: Harper/ Thorsons.

Jukes, A. (1993) *Why Men Hate Women*. London: Free Association Books.

Kernberg, O.F. (1995) *Love Relations: Normality and Pathology.* New Haven, CT: Yale University Press.

Klein, M. (1975) *Love, Guilt and Reparation.* New York: The Free Press.

Klein, M. (1991) 'Early Stages of the Oedipus Conflict.' In J. Mitchell (ed.) *The Selected Melanie Klein.* London: Penguin Books.

Kohut, H. (1977) *The Restoration of the Self.* New York, NY: International Universities Press.

Lacan, J. (1958) 'The Meaning of the Phallus.' in J. Mitchell and J. Rose (eds.) (1982) *Feminine Sexuality.* London: Macmillan.

Lee, D. (2013) 'Do come in… and leave your phone on!' *BACP Children & Young People.*

Lemma, A., Target, M. and Fonagy, P. (2011) *Brief Dynamic Interpersonal Therapy: A Clinician's Guide.* Oxford: Oxford University Press.

Luca, M. (2015, Summer) 'Understanding and handling sexual desire in therapy.' *The Psychotherapist 60.* UKCP.

Luxmoore, N. (2000) *Listening to Young People in School, Youth Work and Counselling.* London: Jessica Kingsley Publishers.

Luxmoore, N. (2006) *Working with Anger and Young People.* London: Jessica Kingsley Publishers.

Luxmoore, N. (2008) *Feeling Like Crap: Young People and the Meaning of Self-esteem.* London: Jessica Kingsley Publishers.

Luxmoore, N. (2010) *Young People in Love and in Hate.* London: Jessica Kingsley Publishers.

Luxmoore, N. (2011) *Young People and the Curse of Ordinariness.* London: Jessica Kingsley Publishers.

Luxmoore, N. (2014) *School Counsellors Working with Young People and Staff: A Whole-school Approach.* London: Jessica Kingsley Publishers.

MacDougall, J. (1995) *The Many Faces of Eros.* London: Free Association Books.

Mann, D. (1995) 'Transference and counter-transference issues with sexually abused clients.' *Psychodynamic Counselling: Individuals, Groups and Organisations 1–4,* 542–559. doi:10.1080/13533339508404153

Mann, D. (1997) *Psychotherapy: An Erotic Relationship.* Hove: Routledge.

Mollon, P. (2001) *Releasing the Self: The Healing Legacy of Heinz Kohut.* London: Whurr Publishers.

Mollon, P. (2002) *Shame and Jealousy: The Hidden Turmoils.* London: Karnac.

Moreno, J.L. (1961) 'The Role Concept, a Bridge Between Psychiatry and Sociology.' In J. Fox (ed.) *The Essential Moreno.* New York, NY: Springer.

Moreno, J.L. (1972) *Psychodrama (Vol. 1).* New York: Beacon House.

Murdin, L. (2000) *How Much Is Enough?* London: Routledge.

Nitsun, M. (2006) *The Group as an Object of Desire.* Hove: Routledge.

Nussbaum, M.C. (2001) *Upheavals of Thought.* Cambridge: Cambridge University Press.

Ogden, T.H. (1986) *The Matrix of the Mind: Object Relations and the Psychoanalytic Dialogue.* Northvale, NJ: Jason Aronson.

Orbach, S. and Eichenbaum, L. (1994) *What Do Women Want?* London: HarperCollins.

Page, S. (1999) *The Shadow and the Counsellor.* London: Routledge.

Pearce, J.J. (2007) 'Sex and Risk.' In J. Coleman and A. Hagell (eds.) *Adolescence, Risk and Resilience.* Chichester: Wiley.

Phillips, A. (1995) *Terrors and Experts.* London: Faber.

Phillips, A. (2005) *Going Sane.* London: Hamish Hamilton.

Phillips, A. (2010) *On Balance.* London: Hamish Hamilton.

Phillips, A. (2012) *Missing Out: In Praise of the Unlived Life.* London: Hamish Hamilton.

Radford, L., Corral, S., Bradley, C., Fisher, H., Bassett, C., Howat, N. and Collishaw, S. (2011) *Child Abuse and Neglect in the UK Today.* London: NSPCC.

Rattigan, B. (2006) 'He or she? Trying to think psychodynamically about a service for people with gender dysphoria' in J. Hiller, H. Wood and W. Bolton (eds.) *Sex, Mind and Emotion.* London: Karnac Books.

Sayers, J. (1998) *Boy Crazy.* London: Routledge.

Schwartz, J. (2007) 'Attachment and Sexuality.' In K. White and J. Schwartz (eds.) *Sexuality and Attachment in Clinical Practice.* London: Karnac Books.

Spinelli, E. (1994) *Demystifying Therapy.* London: Constable and Company.

Spinelli, E. (2001) *The Mirror and the Hammer.* London: Continuum.

Staunton, T. (2002) 'Sexuality and Body Psychotherapy.' In T. Staunton (ed.) *Body Psychotherapy.* Hove: Routledge.

Stern, D.N. (1985) *The Interpersonal World of the Infant.* New York, NY: Basic Books.

Storr, A. (1972) *The Dynamics of Creation.* London: Secker and Warburg.

Suttie, I.D. (1935) *The Origins of Love and Hate*. London: Kegan Paul.

Welldon, E.V. (1988) *Mother, Madonna, Whore: The Idealisation and Denigration of Motherhood*. New York, NY: The Guilford Press.

Winnicott, D.W. (1965) *The Maturational Processes and the Facilitating Environment*. London: Hogarth Press.

Winnicott, D.W. (1971) *Playing and Reality*. London: Routledge.

Winnicott, D.W. (1975) *Through Paediatrics to Psychoanalysis: Collected Papers*. London: Hogarth Press.

Winnicott, D.W. (1989) 'Fear of Breakdown.' In C. Winnicott, R. Shepherd and M. Davis (eds.) *Psycho-Analytic Explorations*. London: Karnac Books.

Yalom, I.D. (1980) *Existential Psychotherapy*. New York, NY: Basic Books.

Yalom, I.D. (1996) *Lying on the Couch*. New York, NY: HarperCollins.

INDEX

abortion 65, 162
abuse 23, 47, 149, 153
    emotional 88
    sexual 36, 174
    verbal 111
acting out 40, 87, 112, 161
advice 19, 129, 142, 178, 204
agency
    sense of 11, 87
    sexual 47
aloneness 23, 68, 95–104, 107, 137, 141,
        170
    existential 104
    sexual 95
    togetherness 100–1
Allison, E. 172
Alvarez, A. 119, 150, 164, 197
ambivalence 37, 48, 126, 165, 169
anger 72, 103, 112, 120, 131, 142–3, 146,
        161, 173, 181–4, 188–9, 191, 194–5,
        197–201, 203–6
anorexia 162
anxiety, anxieties 9, 11, 13–14, 17–18, 27,
        49, 53, 58, 75, 78–9, 81, 95, 97, 99,
        101–2, 111–12, 115, 119, 140, 150,
        160–1, 167–9, 172, 181–2, 184–5,
        187, 189, 203–5, 207
    baby 30
    paedophilic 17
    sexual 30, 34, 36, 40–1
attachment 25, 75, 112, 119, 121, 156, 172,
        176, 178
    contexts 26
    disturbance 26
    early 25
    experience 25
    figure 188
    romantic 184
authenticity 173, 175–6

authority–figures 96

Balint, M. 24
Baron-Cohen, S. 28
Barter, C. 23
bereavement 18
betrayal 13, 67, 74, 77, 87, 131, 133
Bettelheim, B. 30
Bion, W. 176
bisexual(ity) 15, 26–7, 39, 86–7, 115
    psychic 26
blow-job 108, 110–11
body, bodies 14, 24, 37, 71–3, 75–8, 80–2,
        85, 88, 91, 110–11, 132, 159–60, 177
boundaries 44, 126–7, 154–5
Bowlby, J. 25
boys *passim*
    heterosexual 178
    homosexual 178
Bramley, W. 164
breasts 72, 79
Briggs, S. 38
bullying 9, 88, 112, 209
    casual 40
    homophobic 39
    sexualized 40
Butler, J. 28

Chodorow, N. 14–15, 111, 134, 136–7,
        178–9
circumcision 59
clitoris 59
Cohen, J. 109
computer games 21, 141
condom(s) 13–14, 16, 51–3, 55–7, 59–60,
        62
    demonstration 13
confidence 49, 74–7, 80, 89, 92, 109, 124,
        129–30, 135, 139, 184, 193, 197,
        199, 203, 205, 209

confidentiality 67, 117, 194
consent 43, 109
containment 19
contraception 51, 63
control 10, 13, 64, 73, 77, 79, 87, 98,
    103–4, 109, 111, 113–14, 116–17,
    126, 130, 132, 149, 151, 164
core complex 25, 99
counselling, counsellor(s) passim
    relationship(s) 103–4, 156, 163, 170
    room 19, 30, 80, 83, 147, 149, 151–2,
        154, 160, 162–3, 166, 170, 179,
        185, 188, 194
    school 51
Coy, M. 108
creativity 189, 191, 193–4, 197, 200, 203
culture, cultural 41, 72, 178
    background 14, 23
    heterosexual 39
    school 49
    story 14–15
cutting 131

Davies, J.M. 166
De Beauvoir, S. 72–3
defence(s) 53, 117, 119, 121, 155, 169,
    171–2, 175, 177, 179, 197
    narcissistic 179
    sexualized 121
delight 75, 150–1, 155, 168, 170, 179, 188
dependency 14, 27, 98, 115, 132, 178
depression 9, 119, 131, 172, 196, 199, 201
desire 14, 34, 43, 88, 91, 115, 120, 152–4,
    176, 192, 203
    genital 44
    incestuous 166
    sexual 200
developmental object 166
Diamond, N. 25, 111, 119
disappointment(s) 13, 23, 92, 137, 144,
    147, 168, 171, 182, 185–6
discontinuities 92
drugs 165

eating 78–9
ego 25
    ideal 132

Eichenbaum, L. 137
Ellis Nutt, A. 28
embarrassment 22, 36, 42, 51–3, 83, 90,
    130, 141–2, 145, 157, 174, 178, 180,
    195, 200
empathy 113, 119, 122
Ensler, E. 72
epistemic
    trust 172
    vigilance 172
epistemophilic instinct 37
Eros, erotic 38
    feelings 155–6, 159–60
    instinct 200
    interest 156
    love 88
    striving 24
eroticization 119
exam(s) 81, 84, 101, 184, 203–4, 206–7,
    209
    results 34
exploitation 23
Facebook 132
failure(s) 82, 143, 184, 204, 209
family 34, 47–9, 62, 73, 107, 122, 133, 172,
    197, 200, 204
    dynamics 126, 182
    system 182
fantasy 14, 92, 136
father(s) passim
    figure 45, 147, 167
    good 140
    step 45
    transferential 161, 174
    unconscious 49
feelings passim
    erotic 155–6, 159–60
    genital 154
    sexual 44, 71, 155, 176
    split off 81
    unconscious 14
female genital mutilation 59
femininity 111, 179

flirting, flirtation 117, 120–1, 164, 182, 205, 207
Fonagy, P. 26, 172
foreplay 164
    therapeutic 164
Foucault, M. 15
Freud, S. 17, 24, 26, 33, 72, 86, 91, 132, 155, 163, 200
friend(s) *passim*
Frog Prince, The 30
Frosh, S. 24
frustration 25, 64, 78, 92–3, 99, 103, 112, 151, 181, 189, 198

Gabbard, G.O. 155
gang 85
gay 15, 26, 39, 41, 58–9, 61, 86, 115, 158, 193
gender 15–16, 28, 161
    dysphoria 28
    identity 14
    socially constructed 28
genital(s) 24, 28, 44, 59, 113, 154
    desire 44
    feelings 154
Gerhardt, S. 187
Gilligan, J. 79, 109
Glasser, M. 25, 98
Go-Between, The 12
Gomez, L. 24
Graham, P. 40
grandiosity 171
Grease 42
grooming 17, 46
groups, groupwork 13, 27, 39–40, 49
G-spot 59
guilt 140, 174

Hartley, L.P. 12
hatred, hate 33, 68, 71–2, 75, 78–9, 108, 114–15, 118–19, 131, 140–3, 162, 170, 177, 197–8, 203
hedonic intersubjectivity 161
heterosexual 19, 39
    boys 178
    sex 39
hide-and-seek 117 *see also* peek-a-boo

Hiller, J. 15–16
Hines, M. 28
Hines, S. 15
Hobson, R.F. 100
Holmes, J. 161, 172
homophobia 41, 61
homosexual 19
    boys 178
    sex 39
hormones 200
Horne, A. 111
humiliation 109, 111, 113–14, 178, 180, 198
Hurry, A. 166
id 25
    libidinal 38
identity 15, 26, 29–30, 80, 84, 98, 100, 129
    gender 14
impingements 92
impotence 166, 169
independence 27, 98–9, 103, 115, 132, 143, 178
infancy 24, 26, 100, 150
infection 23, 55
innocence 113
instinct
    death 200
    epistemophilic 37
    erotic 200
    for knowledge 37
intermediate space 102
intimacy 14, 44, 47, 97, 99, 109, 113, 129, 141, 154, 167, 177

jealousy 23, 145, 154, 191
    sexual 87
Jensen, F.E. 28
Jukes, A. 113, 124, 140

Kernberg, O.F. 92
Klein, M. 37
Kohut, H. 119–21, 181

Lacan, J. 72
Lee, D. 122
Lemma, A. 121
lesbian 39, 85, 87–8, 178
LGBT 39

libidinal energies 37
Lolita 154
longing 16, 25, 43, 88, 113, 119, 175, 178
loss 23, 125, 130, 171
love 24–5, 30, 33, 37, 46, 55, 58, 62, 65, 68,
     74, 78, 82, 87–91, 114, 119, 136–7,
     140, 145, 147, 169–70, 177, 179,
     202–4, 209
   erotic 88
   life 82
   maternal 178
   parental 150
   sexual 88
lubrication 54
Luca, M. 153, 156
lust 43, 88, 118, 120
Luxmoore, N. 23–4, 27, 29, 39, 49, 58, 80,
     83, 87, 101, 115, 119, 123, 140, 165,
     194, 204

Macbeth 57
MacDougall, J. 26
make-up 36, 38, 77–8, 110, 173, 195–7
Mandela, Nelson 151
Mann, D. 163, 174
marriage 18, 58
masculinity 142, 168, 179
masturbation 25, 57–8, 98, 113, 139, 142
menstruation 132
merger, merging 25, 27, 92, 95, 98–9, 115,
     132
mess 79, 126–7
mirror(ing) 182, 184, 188, 196
   enlivening 197
misogyny 41, 140
mixed feelings 9 *see also* ambivalence
Mollon, P. 120, 122, 125
morality, moral 18
   assumptions 18
   disapproval 23
   injunctions 129
   uncertainty 18
Moreno, J.L. 181, 187
mother(s) *passim*
   environmental 80–1
   figure(s) 101, 179

transferential 168
   unconscious 49
Mother Teresa 151
Murdin, L. 155, 174

narcissism, narcissistic 98
   defence(s) 179
   disturbances 155
neuroscience 15, 28, 187–8
Nitsun, M. 15, 49, 72, 92, 176
Nussbaum, M.C. 88

object
   developmental 166
   love 24
   of desire 176
   physical 91
   sexual, sexualized 84, 179
Oedipal
   attack 168
   battle 141
   conflicts 155
   father-figure 167
   relationship 167
   resolution 166
   satisfaction 166
   triumph 139
Ogden, T.H. 98
Oliver 42
Orbach, S. 137
orgasm 21–2, 34, 53, 56, 82
overdose 62, 64, 67

paedophilic 18, 45
   anxiety 17
Page, S. 152
panic attacks 9, 181, 204
parent(s) *passim*
   anxious 97
   figures 45, 98, 114, 140, 153, 166,
        178, 184
   relationship 31
Pearce, J.J. 19
peek-a-boo 117 *see also* hide-and-seek
penis 55–6, 58–60, 71–2, 111, 179
period 51, 66
Phillips, A. 11, 23, 25, 89, 92, 200

phobias 79
pill 16, 66–7
   emergency 16
play, playfulness 75, 102–3, 151, 155,
   163–4, 166–7, 170, 182, 184, 186–8
   projective 181
pleasure 26
   eroticized 111
   physical 25
   principle 86
polymorphous perverse 26
porn 56–8, 138, 140, 142–3
potency 169
potential 186, 193
   space 102
power, powerlessness 13–14, 83, 103, 121,
   131, 140–1, 143, 151, 168, 183
pregnancy, pregnant 23, 56, 65–7, 86, 134,
   162, 198
priests 44, 154
primary tendency 24
privacy, private 18, 59, 103, 109–10,
   115–18, 121, 124, 126–7, 140
   sexual 116
promiscuity 64
promised land 24
psychoanalysis 155, 175, 188
psychotherapy, psychotherapists 24, 163–4
puberty 72
pubic hair 59

queer 29, 40

Radford, L. 36
rape 108
Rattigan, B. 28
reality principle 86
regression 150
relationship(s) *passim*
   childhood 28
   counselling 103–4, 156, 163, 170
   dynamic 98
   education 58
   formative 147
   here-and-now 83
   heterosexual 19
   homosexual 19
   internalized 119, 181

Oedipal 166–7
   parents' 31
   power 83
   professional 154
   romantic 17, 205
   sexual 14, 19, 62, 99, 138, 145, 160,
   163, 177
   sexualisation of 113
   straight 52
   therapeutic 121, 153, 155, 174
   trusting 18
   with parents 24
repression 38
repulsion 16, 154, 156
   sexual 154
resistance 155, 170
revenge 20, 88, 183, 198
rivalry 13, 30
role(s) 30, 43, 181–9, 193, 205

satisfaction(s) 92, 103, 166, 200
   Oedipal 166
   sexual 46
Sayers, J. 178
school(s) *passim*
Schwartz, J. 75, 159
secrecy, secret(s) 85, 127
self 109, 119, 122–3
   actualization 186
   authentic 187
   biopsychosocial 16
   core 119
   disclosure
   esteem 38
   false 121–2
   grown up 198
   harm 78
   idealized 132
   objects 119
   playful child 166
   private 117
   quintessential 186
   real 121–2
   sullen teenager 166
   true 186
semen 56, 77, 126
sensuality 26, 161

separation 25, 27, 92, 98, 111, 115, 132,
      140, 142, 183
sex *passim*
   anal 60–1
   before marriage 18
   change 27
   coercive 19
   consensual 66, 108
   education 38–40, 49, 57–9, 61
   good enough 143
   heterosexual 39
   homosexual 18, 39
   lives 14, 23, 38
   loving 19, 55, 138
   oral 60
   recreational 18
   safe 155
   single 38
   therapists 18
   underage 18
sexual 36, 158
   abuse 19, 23, 36, 47
   activity 163
   adventure 179
   agency 47, 87
   aloneness 95
   anxieties 30, 34, 36, 40–1
   attraction 154
   balancing 42
   beauty 45
   behaviour 17, 129
   beings 26, 36, 47, 129
   bodies 111
   boundaries 140
   business 109
   component 172
   confidence 34, 122, 129
   continuum 15, 44
   curiosity 34
   defence 121
   desire 19, 120, 200
   discovery 24
   exchange 151
   experience(s) 15–17, 26, 37, 40–1,
      91–2, 172

exploitation 17, 23
expressiveness 199, 205
fantasy 14
feelings 44, 71, 155, 176
foreplay 164
free-for-all 37
frustration 34
health 51, 66
histories 176
identities 15, 26, 109, 129
images 14
inadequacy 141
innocence 41
innuendo 38
intercourse 152, 163
jealousy 87
journey 129
knowledge 37
language 111
love 14, 88
needs 86
object 179
option 42
orientation 16–17, 26
outcome 46
part 84
partner 25
person 110
potential 14
practices 61
privacy 116
recovery 24
relationships 19–20, 23–4, 39, 43–4,
      51–2, 58, 62, 64, 71, 89, 95, 99,
      138, 145, 160, 163
remarks 38
repertoire 61
repulsion 154
satisfaction 46
suggestion 118
swearing 38
titillation 119
touch 38
uncertainties 87
undercurrent 33, 41

uneasiness 160

violence 23

sexuality 11–18, 23–6, 28, 30, 37–8, 41–2, 45, 47–9, 71, 76, 82, 89, 92, 109, 136, 139, 143, 149, 151–2, 154–6, 160–3, 169–70, 174, 184, 191, 197

    expressed 160

    genital 151

    socially constructed 15

shame, shaming 16, 41–2, 45, 48, 79, 82, 87, 109–10, 112, 117, 122, 124–5, 153–4, 168, 171, 174, 179, 194, 199

shyness 72, 98, 182, 193

siblings 12, 119, 131–2, 171, 182

silence 100, 104, 146, 182

smegma 55

social workers 44

Spinelli, E. 91, 149

splitting 81, 115, 140, 199

spontaneity 48, 170, 188

spots 79–80

Staunton, T. 156, 161

Stern, D.N. 75

Storr, A. 203

straight 15, 26, 52, 54, 58, 61, 86–7, 115, 158

stress 18

suicide 124–5

superego 25, 142, 155

    anti-libidinal 38

supervision, supervisor 149, 157–9, 162

Suttie, I.D. 45

teacher(s) *passim*

testosterone 113

Thanatos 38

therapeutic alliance 156–7, 161

transference 161, 168, 175–6

    counter 152, 155, 160–1, 176

    erotic 152, 155, 159–60

    father 161, 174

    mother 168

    somatic 161

transgender 29, 39

    issues 28

trauma 18

trust 23, 86, 91, 97, 99, 109–10, 116–17, 121, 129–30, 149, 153–4, 164, 180

Twernlow, S.W. 155

unconscious 176, 182, 198

    attempt 24

    communication 143

    conflict 9, 203

    factors 162

    father 49

    fears 14

    feelings 14

    life 109

    method 143

    mother 49

    processes 159

    reminders 95

    sexual anxieties 30

urethra 59

vagina 54–6, 72

    discharge 55

vibrator 13–14

violence 23, 140, 165, 169

wanking, wanker 52, 58–9, 98

Welldon, E.V. 86

Winnicott, D.W. 26, 80, 92, 95–6, 102–3, 117, 121, 140, 143, 164, 168, 187–8, 193

Yalom, I.D. 98, 152

young people *passim*

youth centre 13

youth worker 13, 44

CPI Antony Rowe
Eastbourne, UK
June 20, 2023